ETHICS DESK REFERENCE for Counselors

Jeffrey E. Barnett and W. Brad Johnson

AMERICAN COUNSELING ASSOCIATION
5999 Stevenson Avenue
Alexandria, VA 22304
www.counseling.org

ETHICS DESK REFERENCE for Counselors

10 9 8 7 6 5 4 3 2 1

American Counseling Association
5999 Stevenson Avenue
Alexandria, VA 22304

Director of Publications Carolyn C. Baker

Production Manager Bonny E. Gaston

Copy Editor Elaine Dunn

Editorial Assistant Catherine A. Brumley

Text and cover design by Bonny E. Gaston.

Library of Congress Cataloging-in-Publication Data

Barnett, Jeffrey E.
Ethics desk reference for counselors/Jeffrey E. Barnett and W. Brad Johnson.
p. cm.
Includes bibliographical references and index.
ISBN 978-1-55620-298-8 (alk. paper)
1. Counselors—Professional ethics. 2. Counseling—Moral and ethical aspects.
3. Counseling—Standards. I. Johnson, W. Brad. II. Title.
BF636.67.B37 2010
174'.91583—dc22 2009015061

Dedication

To our counseling graduate students, past and present

Contents

Appendix

Foreword

Drs. Jeffrey Barnett and Brad Johnson, two highly regarded ethics scholars in the counseling field, have done a marvelous job of interpreting and applying the American Counseling Association (ACA) *Code of Ethics* to a range of counseling settings. Their book is organized in a clear and logical manner, which provides for useful comparisons of the various ethical standards. Each of the standards (or a group of related standards) is followed with a brief section, Essential Elements. This section captures in a nutshell the intent of a given standard or set of standards. There is a Common Dilemmas and Conflicts section that nicely lists some potential risks and areas of concern. The next section, Prevention and Positive Practice, gives a useful checklist of key points that can assist students and counseling practitioners to apply ethical principles to their work. These points are clear and highlight steps leading toward aspirational practice. I found the main points listed in all of these sections to be insightful, and they offer a good platform for further thinking about applying a set of ethical standards to one's own practice situation.

The authors make it clear that the *ACA Code of Ethics* does not address every potential ethical dilemma a counselor is likely to face. With this in mind, they emphasize the importance of developing an approach to ethical decision making as counselors work through an ethical dilemma. I like that the authors highlight that many ethical dilemmas do not have a clearly right or wrong answer. They emphasize the importance of carefully considering what the *ACA Code of Ethics* states as applied to a range of practical situations. A major portion of the book deals with making the best ethical decisions associated with a variety of practice areas, some of which include ethical issues pertaining to culture and diversity, confidentiality and its exceptions, boundaries and multiple relationships, competence, working with clients who are suicidal, supervision, and termination and abandonment. They also address the topic of responding to subpoenas and court orders, lawsuits, and ethics complaints. In each of these areas, the authors have written a concise, clear, and meaningful summary of the topic. I particularly like that they are not rule-bound in their discussion of these topics but have managed to present a balanced discussion of key principles to consider. For example, in writing about multiple relationships, they do identify some of the potential problem areas and offer wisdom to consider before engaging in these relationships. However, they do not judge all such relationships as unethical and unprofessional. In fact, they make the excellent point that sometimes it is possible to harm a client by rigidly adhering to a set of ethical standards without carefully reflecting on the application of these standards to a diverse range of cases.

The writing is exceptionally clear and without extraneous discussion. The authors keep the focus on basic ethical issues and have achieved balanced perspective in discussing various ethical practices. For example, they provide both benefits and risks of engaging in certain ethical practices, such as bartering, forming multiple relationships with clients, and deciding whether or not to accept a client's gift. In the section on ethical issues regarding culture and diversity, they capture the essence of the various ACA standards associated with diversity perspectives. The authors address the problem of being culturally encapsulated and make a number of useful recommendations for practitioners in ethically and effectively providing services to diverse client populations. They underscore the importance of counselors striving to increase their cultural competence, examining their own cultural values, and adapting their counseling practices to a wide range of clients. They have done a fine job of incorporating the theme of multicultural and diversity perspectives that is a part of the 2005 version of the *ACA Code of Ethics* in all the sections in this book.

Readers who want to reflect on questions such as the following will find plenty of thoughtful material to assist them in applying the ethical standards to various practice problems in professional practice:

- How can counselors embrace a multicultural perspective in all aspects of their practice?
- What are some steps counselors can take in thinking through ethical problems they will encounter in their practice?
- What is the role of consultation in working through an ethical dilemma?
- How can informed consent be designed to meet the needs of a wide range of clients from diverse cultural populations?
- What are some ethical dilemmas in assigning a diagnosis to clients from certain cultural groups?
- What are some ethical, cultural, and clinical issues to consider with respect to receiving gifts and bartering?
- What is competence and how can it best be developed and maintained?
- What are some ethical issues to consider in the practice of supervision?
- How can termination of a counseling relationship be done in an ethical and effective manner?

- What are some ways that counselors might respond to a malpractice suit or an ethics complaint?

The authors did not write a book focused on legal issues, nor did they take a legalistic, risk-management approach to ethics. However, their writing reflects the importance of considering the interface of legal and ethical issues in counseling practice, and they do provide specific guidelines that are bound to be good risk-management practices. The authors clearly focus on what is best for clients and what constitutes sound practice. They focus on the best principles of applying ethical standards to a range of problems counselors will need to grapple with, and they challenge the reader to think about the best way to proceed. It is quite clear that Drs. Barnett and Johnson have a clear grasp of ethical practice in counseling and are able to communicate to both students and professional counselors in a collegial manner. They avoid being prescriptive, and at the same time, they offer some solid advice for students and counselors to consider in their process of ethical decision making. I would see this book as being a useful supplementary book for students in ethics courses and for counseling professionals in a variety of specializations. The book is a useful reference tool that can be consulted at various points in conjunction with consulting with trusted colleagues. Furthermore, the book is easy to read, is interesting, and provides food for thought.

—Gerald Corey, EdD

Diplomate in Counseling Psychology, ABPP
Professor Emeritus of Human Services and Counseling
California State University, Fullerton

Preface

Counselors strive to practice ethically and competently, with the best interests of those they serve in mind. The American Counseling Association (ACA) *Code of Ethics* is the primary source of guidance for ethical practice by counselors. It applies to all roles, settings, and types of services counselors provide. While some aspects of the *ACA Code of Ethics* may seem straightforward, even obvious, in application, other aspects of the *Code of Ethics* may leave counselors feeling perplexed about how best to apply them. The *Ethics Desk Reference for Counselors* (*EDR*) is designed to assist counselors in both the interpretation and application of the *ACA Code of Ethics.* Each section of the *Code of Ethics* is reprinted here accompanied by a brief commentary that emphasizes its most essential elements, common ethical dilemmas and problems relevant to that section, and specific strategies for prevention and positive practice. While the *ACA Code of Ethics* provides standards and guidance relevant to all aspects of each counselor's professional activities and context, it cannot provide specific guidance or concrete answers for every situation or ethical dilemma. Therefore, we provide a decision-making model to assist counselors in applying the *ACA Code of Ethics* to the broad range of challenges and situations faced in the course of their work. This model provides a step-by-step process for responding thoughtfully to dilemmas that may confront counselors and is intended to supplement the use of the *ACA Code of Ethics.*

Counselors work in a wide range of roles and settings with diverse clients, supervisees, students, research participants, and colleagues. As a counselor, you may face a host of quandaries and dilemmas in your counseling practice, your supervisory work, your teaching, your research, and even your collegial relationships. A thorough understanding of the *ACA Code of Ethics* and how to effectively apply it in any situation will help ensure that you provide the best possible professional services. Let's be clear, no one can expect to handle every ethical dilemma flawlessly; life and counseling work are simply too complicated for that. But the use of a thoughtful decision-making process, consultation with colleagues, knowledge of relevant laws, regulations and policies, and the effective application of the *ACA Code of Ethics* each will contribute to ethical conduct and practice.

The *EDR* is intended to be an easy-to-use and accessible resource for every counselor and for every counselor-in-training. In addition to explaining each section of the *ACA Code of Ethics*, its application, dilemmas associated with it, and proven strategies for prevention and positive practice, the *EDR* offers a number of additional resources to assist counselors in their work. Part II of the *EDR* provides specific ethical guidance in key areas of counseling that are most likely to provoke ethical questions and dilemmas. These special guidance sections include ethical issues in culture and diversity, confidentiality, exceptions to confidentiality, counseling suicidal clients, boundaries and multiple relationships in counseling, competence, supervision, managed care, termination and abandonment, and how to respond to an ethics complaint or malpractice suit. Finally, we provide a set of resources to augment the *EDR* and provide counselors with further consultation and study in the area of professional ethics.

We hope that the *EDR* will be an indispensable resource for each counselor and each counselor-in-training. We also hope you will keep it on your desk, refer to it frequently, and utilize its guidance to help promote ethical and effective counseling practice on an ongoing basis.

Finally, we express our great thanks to Carolyn Baker, the Director of Publications at the American Counseling Association. Carolyn was extremely helpful in assisting us in taking the *EDR* from our initial idea to this published final product. Carolyn was a valued resource who assisted us each step along the way with her support, guidance, and thoughtful feedback.

About the Authors

Jeffrey E. Barnett, PsyD, ABPP, is a licensed mental health professional and a professor at Loyola University, Maryland. There, among other duties, he trains master's-level students in counseling psychology and advanced graduate students in the Licensed Clinical Professional Counselor track. He has served on professional ethics committees and regularly publishes and presents in the areas of ethics, legal, and professional practice issues for mental health professionals. Additionally, he serves in various editorial capacities for a number of professional publications. His most recent book is *Financial Success in Mental Health Practice: Essential Strategies and Tools* (2008; with Steven Walfish).

W. Brad Johnson, PhD, teaches in the counseling program in the Graduate School of Education at Johns Hopkins University, where he is a faculty associate. He is also a professor at the U.S. Naval Academy. He has authored more than 90 articles and book chapters, as well as 10 books, in the areas of ethical behavior, mentor relationships, and counseling. Among his most recent books are *The Elements of Ethics* (2008; with Charles Ridley), *The Elements of Mentoring: Revised Edition* (2008; with Charles Ridley), and *Write to the Top: How to Become a Prolific Academic* (2007; with Carol Mullen).

PART I

The American Counseling Association *Code of Ethics*

Section A

The Counseling Relationship

Introduction

Counselors encourage client growth and development in ways that foster the interest and welfare of clients and promote formation of healthy relationships. Counselors actively attempt to understand the diverse cultural backgrounds of the clients they serve.

Counselors also explore their own cultural identities and how these affect their values and beliefs about the counseling process. Counselors are encouraged to contribute to society by devoting a portion of their professional activity to services for which there is little or no financial return (pro bono publico).

Essential Elements

Counselors are mindful of their role with clients and the potential impact their actions may have on clients. Therefore, counselors give careful thought and consideration to how they interact with clients with a specific focus on each client's welfare, only acting in ways that are consistent with clients' best interests. Counselors pursue the overarching goal of helping clients to develop and maintain healthy relationships in their lives. This begins with the counseling relationship. Counselors give careful attention to diversity issues, thoughtfully considering the impact of culture on themselves, their clients, and all interactions with clients. Because of a lifelong commitment to the betterment of others and to assist those without ready access to needed counseling services, counselors are encouraged to offer services to some reasonable portion of their clients either free or for a reduced fee as they are financially able to.

Common Dilemmas and Conflicts

- Counselors who become preoccupied or distracted by personal needs or concerns may lose sight of the best interests of their clients.
- Counselors who limit their focus to the treatment of symptoms or disorders may neglect the essential focus on the promotion of healthy relationships.
- A lack of self-reflection and self-awareness regarding one's own cultural background and identities may result in harm to the counseling relationship and to clients.
- Counselors who overlook the potential impact of their own values and beliefs may be less effective in helping clients.
- Counselors who believe there is a mandate to treat clients free or for a reduced fee may experience financial hardship, resentment of clients, and, therefore, poor counseling outcomes.

Prevention and Positive Practice

✓ Always consider each client's best interests and the potential impact of your actions on clients before acting.
✓ Intentionally use the counseling relationship to model healthy and appropriate interactions for clients to emulate in other relationships in their lives.
✓ Always treat clients with respect and dignity.
✓ Carefully consider the role of personal values and beliefs to ensure that your own goals and values are not inadvertently imposed on clients.
✓ Consider the role of culture and other aspects of diversity—such as ethnicity, age, gender, religion, and sexual orientation—in your assessments, interventions, and relationships with clients.
✓ Aspire to donate some portion of your professional services to clients who would not otherwise be able to afford them.

A.1. Welfare of Those Served by Counselors

A.1.a. Primary Responsibility

> The primary responsibility of counselors is to respect the dignity and to promote the welfare of clients.

Essential Elements

Above all else, counselors strive to communicate respect and appreciation for each client's worthiness, value, and autonomy. Honoring dignity is imperative regardless of the client's behavior or circumstances. In addition, counselors must deliberately work to promote the best interests, happiness, and health of those they serve.

Common Dilemmas and Conflicts

- Counselors who focus primarily on their own needs and interests may act in ways that conflict with clients' welfare and best interests.

- When experiencing a conflict or disagreement with a client, counselors may be tempted to treat clients in disrespectful or abusive ways.
- Counselors who are unfamiliar with or inattentive to a client's cultural experience may inadvertently communicate disrespect or disregard.

Prevention and Positive Practice

✓ Always consider the potential impact of your interactions with clients.
✓ Diligently work to accord dignity to clients by communicating respect and engaging each client as a person of great value and worth.
✓ Before taking an action, ask yourself if it is consistent with the overarching ideals of the counseling profession and if it will help promote the client's welfare.
✓ Communicate dignity and respect by engaging clients in all phases of decision making regarding the counseling plan and process *(see A.1.c.).*
✓ Find ways to communicate interest in and respect for each client's cultural identity *(see A.2.c, B.1.a.).*

A.1.b. Records

Counselors maintain records necessary for rendering professional services to their clients and as required by laws, regulations, or agency or institution procedures. Counselors include sufficient and timely documentation in their client records to facilitate the delivery and continuity of needed services. Counselors take reasonable steps to ensure that documentation in records accurately reflects client progress and services provided. If errors are made in client records, counselors take steps to properly note the correction of such errors according to agency or institutional policies. *(See A.12.g.7., B.6., B.6.g., G.2.j.)*

Essential Elements

Documentation and record keeping are essential elements of every professional counseling relationship. There are several reasons for thorough and timely documentation of counseling services. These include (a) abiding by the relevant laws, regulations, and requirements of a counseling work setting; (b) facilitating seamless ongoing counseling; (c) communicating with colleagues when working with a client in a team treatment setting; (d) smoothing reentry should a client return to counseling at a later date; and (e) facilitating continuity should you need to transfer a client's care to another provider or agency. Thorough documentation also provides the tangible record of a counselor's good-faith efforts to provide clients with the best possible care. It may serve an effective risk management function should questions ever arise about counseling services provided to a client. As such, all documentation should be accurate and honest, clearly noting services provided, each participant's role in the counseling relationship, and results achieved. If changes need to be made to the record because of an error or oversight, the corrections should be made in a manner that clearly indicates the date and rationale for the change.

Common Dilemmas and Conflicts

- Busy counselors may be tempted to delay documentation and suffer the effects of the passage of time on their memory, negatively affecting the thoroughness and accuracy of the record.
- Counselors who fail to anticipate the many ways a record may be used in the future may insufficiently document their work, resulting in potential harm to clients.
- Counselors who overlook their particular agency's documentation requirements may inadvertently violate institutional policies despite their efforts to effectively document services provided.
- After documentation of a particular session is complete, if a counselor remembers important information to include in the record, it may be tempting to try to insert the additional information in the record as though it were part of the original documentation.
- Counselors may be tempted to dispose of records prematurely when they believe that a client will not return for additional services.

Prevention and Positive Practice

✓ Maintain records for all clients in accordance with relevant laws and regulations in your jurisdiction and the policies in your workplace.
✓ Carefully consider the potential uses of a record in the future when making decisions about documentation and information to be included.
✓ Attend to confidentiality issues when documenting, storing records, determining access to records, and disposing of records (*see Section B.6. for detailed guidance regarding confidentiality and record keeping*).
✓ Whenever documentation occurs at a time other than when the service is provided, this should be noted clearly in the record.
✓ In addition to documenting the services provided, the client's role, progress achieved, recommendations made, and the like, it is important to include the rationale behind all counseling treatment decisions.

A.1.c. Counseling Plans

> Counselors and their clients work jointly in devising integrated counseling plans that offer reasonable promise of success and are consistent with abilities and circumstances of clients. Counselors and clients regularly review counseling plans to assess their continued viability and effectiveness, respecting the freedom of choice of clients. *(See A.2.a., A.2.d., A.12.g.)*

Essential Elements

Counselors adopt a collaborative approach in their work with clients. Counselors thoughtfully assess each client's needs at the outset of the professional relationship; carefully consider the client's unique needs, abilities, and circumstances; and then work with clients to create a counseling plan consistent with these factors. Counselors involve clients in formulating, executing, and frequently revisiting and updating the counseling plan as the client's needs, circumstances, and preferences warrant. Counselors help clients to understand what plans and approaches are likely to yield the greatest benefit for the client, and counselors remain ever mindful of each client's autonomy, the client's right to make important counseling decisions, and the client's right to refuse recommendations and discontinue counseling at any time.

Common Dilemmas and Conflicts

- Failure to assess each client's strengths, needs, and goals at the outset of the counseling relationship may result in harm to the client.
- Setting goals that are not reasonable or realistic when considering the client's abilities and circumstances may undermine the success of a counseling plan.
- Selecting goals and developing a counseling plan unilaterally—without client collaboration—diminishes the client's autonomy, may fail to promote the client's welfare *(see A.1.a.)*, and could risk superseding the client's values and goals (*see Introduction*).
- Failure to reassess and update the counseling plan over the course of the counseling relationship can reduce the effectiveness of care.

Prevention and Positive Practice

✓ Thoroughly assess each client's counseling needs, goals, assets, and liabilities from the outset of the counseling relationship.
✓ Always ensure that this is a collaborative process and actively work to incorporate the client's wishes and expectations into the counseling plan.
✓ Regularly review progress with the client and, together, revise and update the counseling plan as is needed.
✓ Attend to factors that may affect goal setting in the counseling relationship, such as financial and insurance limitations, client motivation, and the client's level of support.

A.1.d. Support Network Involvement

Counselors recognize that support networks hold various meanings in the lives of clients and consider enlisting the support, understanding, and involvement of others (e.g., religious/spiritual/community leaders, family members, friends) as positive resources, when appropriate, with client consent.

Essential Elements

Counselors understand the inherently relational nature of the counseling process and that the relationships in each client's life may be significant resources for the client. When therapeutically appropriate, and after open discussion with the client, it may be important to access these relationship resources—with the client's informed consent—to enlist their aid and support for the client. It is important to see significant others in a client's life as potential resources to be tapped in order to support the client in the counseling process. Counselors should be knowledgeable about the varied support networks in each client's life and, when appropriate, assist the client to enlist and utilize their support *(see A.2.c.)*.

Common Dilemmas and Conflicts

- Assuming that the counseling relationship is all the client needs to achieve counseling treatment goals is shortsighted and very limiting.
- Failure to help clients reach out and enlist the support of others may undermine the contributions of relational networks that could help clients move toward their goals.
- It may be tempting to assume that certain individuals or groups in a client's life will exert either a negative or a positive influence on the client; making assumptions about these entities without exploring their role in the client's life may result in valuable resources being overlooked.
- Counselors who become defensive about the involvement of others in the counseling process or who harbor negative views about specific networks (e.g., religious organizations) may fail to maximize a client's support.

Prevention and Positive Practice

✓ Always consider the client's support network as a potential resource for buttressing and reinforcing the work of the counseling relationship.

✓ Discuss openly with clients who may be a good resource and how and when to enlist their involvement in and support of the counseling process *(see A.1.c.)*.

✓ Only contact support network members with the client's permission through informed consent.

✓ Monitor the effectiveness and value of these resources for the client and openly discuss your observations with the client.

A.1.e. Employment Needs

> Counselors work with their clients considering employment in jobs that are consistent with the overall abilities, vocational limitations, physical restrictions, general temperament, interest and aptitude patterns, social skills, education, general qualifications, and other relevant characteristics and needs of clients. When appropriate, counselors appropriately trained in career development will assist in the placement of clients in positions that are consistent with the interest, culture, and the welfare of clients, employers, and/or the public.

Essential Elements

Many counselors assist clients with employment decisions and, when they have the needed competence, with career development issues. In keeping with the general obligation to promote each client's welfare *(see A.1.a.)*, counselors consider all relevant factors prior to making employment recommendations. These relevant factors include, but may not be limited to, the client's culture, abilities, vocational limitations, physical restrictions, general temperament, interest and aptitude patterns, social skills, education, and general qualifications. The potential impact of particular vocational recommendations and job placements on the client, employers, and the public should be considered.

Common Dilemmas and Conflicts

- Counselors without specific expertise in vocational counseling may go beyond the limits of their competence and make recommendations inconsistent with a client's best interests.
- Failure to consider the full range of vocational and cultural factors may result in poor job placement decisions.
- Insensitivity to clients' strengths, interests, and limitations may result in job placements that are a poor fit for the client.
- A desire to help a client find employment quickly may result in poor long-term outcomes.

Prevention and Positive Practice

✓ Counselors should develop the needed competence in vocational counseling and career development—through course work, workshops, training, and supervised experience—prior to working with clients in this area of counseling practice *(see C.2.)*.

✓ Each client should be comprehensively assessed—with regard to interests, preferences, aptitudes, strengths, limitations, and any other variables relevant to vocational functioning—prior to making any vocational recommendations.

✓ Goodness of fit and long-term success should be salient priorities in vocational counseling assessments and decisions.

A.2. Informed Consent in the Counseling Relationship *(See A.12.g., B.5., B.6.b., E.3., E.13.b., F.1.c., G.2.a.)*

A.2.a. Informed Consent

> Clients have the freedom to choose whether to enter into or remain in a counseling relationship and need adequate information about the counseling process and the counselor. Counselors have an obligation to review in writing and verbally with clients the rights and responsibilities of both the counselor and the client. Informed consent is an ongoing part of the counseling process, and counselors appropriately document discussions of informed consent throughout the counseling relationship.

Essential Elements

Informed consent in the counseling relationship promotes respect, autonomy, and the client's best interests *(see Introduction and A.1.a.)*. Informed consent involves providing clients with sufficient information so they may make a reasoned decision about participation in the counseling relationship. Informed consent should be viewed as an ongoing process rather than a single event. Clients have the right to know all relevant information about the counselor, such as relevant experience, credentials, and training. Additionally, they should be fully informed about anything that might reasonably be expected to affect their decision to participate in the counseling relationship, such as fees, scheduling, potential risks and benefits, specific services to be provided, goals, and the like. All informed consent agreements should be reviewed verbally to ensure clients' understanding of them and should also be documented as part of the treatment record *(see A.1.b., A.1.c.)*.

Common Dilemmas and Conflicts

- Having clients read and sign a written informed consent agreement without discussing the agreement and ensuring their understanding does not achieve the goals of this standard.
- Viewing client questions about one's qualifications, credentials, the course of treatment, or billing practices as intrusive or challenging of one's expertise will likely minimize the value of the informed consent agreement.
- Counselors who see informed consent as an onerous burden or a single event to be hurried through in the first session may be at risk of minimizing the potential benefits of informed consent for clients.
- Counselors who take an authoritarian—as opposed to collaborative—stance may violate the voluntary nature of informed consent and be coercive in this process.

Prevention and Positive Practice

✓ Always consider informed consent an integral element of every counseling relationship.
✓ Ensure that consent is given freely and that this is a voluntary process.
✓ Ensure that clients receive all information needed to make an informed decision about participation in the counseling relationship.
✓ Share information with clients both verbally and in writing. Include all written informed consent agreements in the treatment record.
✓ Update the informed consent agreement with clients on an ongoing basis and whenever significant changes in the counseling process are being considered.

A.2.b. Types of Information Needed

Counselors explicitly explain to clients the nature of all services provided. They inform clients about issues such as, but not limited to, the following: the purposes, goals, techniques, procedures, limitations, potential risks, and benefits of services; the counselor's qualifications, credentials, and relevant experience; continuation of services upon the incapacitation or death of a counselor; and other pertinent information. Counselors take steps to ensure that clients understand the implications of diagnosis, the intended use of tests and reports, fees, and billing arrangements. Clients have the right to confidentiality and to be provided with an explanation of its limitations (including how supervisors and/or treatment team professionals are involved); to obtain clear information about their records to participate in the ongoing counseling plans; and to refuse any services or modality change and to be advised of the consequences of such refusal.

Essential Elements

Counselors deliberately provide clients with a full range of information needed to assist them in making an informed decision about participating in the counseling relationship. Salient information includes the purposes, goals, techniques, procedures, limitations, potential risks, and benefits of participation in the counseling relationship as well as fees and billing, assessments, and use of formal diagnoses. Additionally, counselors must share their qualifications, credentials, and professional experience relevant to the particular client's counseling needs *(see C.4.)*. Information about arrangements for meeting the client's counseling needs should the counselor not be able to continue the relationship should be addressed as well. Clients are informed about confidentiality *(see B.1.)* and any limits to it that may be reasonably anticipated *(see B.2.)*, as well as the voluntary nature of their participation in the counseling relationship, their right to withdraw or refuse certain services, and any implications of these decisions.

Common Dilemmas and Conflicts

- Counselors who assume that clients are knowledgeable about the counseling process may neglect to provide them with important information.
- Failure to anticipate potential problems, developments, and changes in the counseling relationship can result in inadequate informed consent.
- Counselors who are authoritarian, controlling, or defensive may minimize this process and harm the counseling relationship.

Prevention and Positive Practice

✓ Develop an informed consent checklist specific to your counseling setting to ensure that all relevant information is shared with clients.
✓ Provide sufficient information relevant to each individual client's situation and needs so the client may make an informed decision about participation.
✓ Discuss all reasonably anticipated limits to confidentiality with clients, including the roles of supervisors and treatment team members.
✓ Ensure that clients understand all their rights regarding participation in treatment, decision making, accessing records, and refusal of treatment.
✓ Recognize that every counseling relationship is fluid and that new information will become pertinent to informed consent as each relationship evolves.
✓ Be certain that clients understand the myriad ways in which assessment data and evaluation results may be used.

A.2.c. Developmental and Cultural Sensitivity

Counselors communicate information in ways that are both developmentally and culturally appropriate. Counselors use clear and understandable language when discussing issues related to informed consent. When clients have difficulty understanding the language used by counselors, they provide necessary services (e.g., arranging for a qualified interpreter or translator) to ensure comprehension by clients. In collaboration with clients, counselors consider cultural implications of informed consent procedures and, where possible, counselors adjust their practices accordingly.

Essential Elements

Sharing information with clients as part of the informed consent process must be done in a way that promotes the client's full understanding. Counselors must carefully attend to developmental issues (e.g., intellectual capabilities, communication difficulties) and diversity issues (e.g., language ability, fluency) when sharing information with clients. Translators should be used as appropriate, and information should be shared with clients in a manner that will be comprehensible to them. Counselors should actively consider how culture and other diversity factors may affect the informed consent process for clients and adjust their practices accordingly. For instance, clients from some cultural backgrounds may prefer that a senior family member give consent for counseling services *(see B.1.a.)*.

Common Dilemmas and Conflicts

- Counselors who overlook the role of developmental variables and diversity factors risk an ineffective informed consent process.
- Failure to attend to the client's ability to comprehend information—verbally or in writing—may result in the misunderstanding of key information.
- Counselors who use professional jargon risk having clients fail to understand what they are agreeing to.

Prevention and Positive Practice

✓ Always assess each client's language, intellectual, communication, and other developmental capacities that may affect their understanding and participation in the informed consent process.
✓ Present information (whether verbally or in writing) to clients at a level that they can understand.
✓ Actively ensure each client's understanding of the information you share with them.
✓ Ensure that diversity factors are considered throughout the informed consent process and modify practices and procedures as needed.
✓ Make necessary arrangements, such as use of a translator or interpreter, to ensure each client's full comprehension of the information you share with the client.

A.2.d. Inability to Give Consent

> When counseling minors or persons unable to give voluntary consent, counselors seek the assent of clients to services, and include them in decision making as appropriate. Counselors recognize the need to balance the ethical rights of clients to make choices, their capacity to give consent or assent to receive services, and parental or familial legal rights and responsibilities to protect these clients and make decisions on their behalf.

Essential Elements

Minors and others who are unable to legally provide informed consent (e.g., elderly clients with cognitive impairment, clients with developmental disability) should nonetheless be included in the informed consent process as fully as is feasible. They should be informed of relevant information about their counseling even if they are not legally or otherwise capable of consenting to counseling.

Counselors seek to promote clients' rights and best interests even in those situations when they are not able to provide voluntary informed consent on their own behalf. In these situations, counselors seek collaborative relationships with clients' legal custodians and, whenever possible, work to balance the rights of clients with those of their legal guardians. Counselors maintain current knowledge of and abide by relevant state or provincial laws bearing on the rights of juveniles to seek treatment and give informed consent, as well as requirements for parental informed consent *(see B.5., H.1.b.)*.

Common Dilemmas and Conflicts

- Sharing information exclusively with parents or other legal guardians may result in clients' rights being violated and an ineffective counseling relationship.
- Failure to actively involve clients in the decision-making process may promote dependency, feelings of alienation, or lack of full participation in counseling.
- Confusion over who the actual client is, who holds legal authority to grant consent, and each party's assorted rights may result in a poor outcome.

Prevention and Positive Practice

✓ Clarify each person's legal rights and your obligations to each from the outset.
✓ Include each client in the decision-making process as fully as possible and attempt to obtain the client's assent to the counseling relationship.
✓ Be sure that voluntary informed consent is obtained from an individual legally authorized to provide it before beginning a counseling relationship.

A.3. Clients Served by Others

When counselors learn that their clients are in a professional relationship with another mental health professional, they request release from clients to inform the other professionals and strive to establish positive and collaborative professional relationships.

Essential Elements

For a variety of reasons, clients may simultaneously be in a professional relationship with other mental health professionals. Counselors should always ask about this, and when such co-occurring relationships are revealed, they should obtain the client's permission and then contact the other professional so that all professional services may be coordinated to maximize the client's best interests and minimize conflict or misunderstanding *(see Section D)*.

Common Dilemmas and Conflicts

- Clients may not spontaneously share about other professional relationships.
- Failure to coordinate care with other treating professionals may result in each working at cross-purposes with the other.

- Failure to obtain information from other treating professionals may result in the counselor proceeding without potentially valuable information relevant to the client and the counseling relationship.
- Counselors who become defensive or competitive with other professionals may fail to collaborate effectively on their clients' behalf.

Prevention and Positive Practice

✓ Include questions about other professional relationships in the initial interview with all clients and update this as needed over time.
✓ Include permission to contact and share information with other treating professionals in each client's informed consent agreement.
✓ See other professionals as resources who may have valuable information to share that can contribute to the success of the counseling relationship.

A.4. Avoiding Harm and Imposing Values

A.4.a. Avoiding Harm

Counselors act to avoid harming their clients, trainees, and research participants and to minimize or to remedy unavoidable or unanticipated harm.

A.4.b. Personal Values

Counselors are aware of their own values, attitudes, beliefs, and behaviors and avoid imposing values that are inconsistent with counseling goals. Counselors respect the diversity of clients, trainees, and research participants.

Essential Elements

In their efforts to be of assistance to clients, trainees, and research participants, counselors work to anticipate possible sources of harm and seek to actively prevent them when possible and to minimize their impact when they cannot be avoided *(see A.1.a.)*. Counselors attend to their personal values, attitudes, beliefs, and behaviors and work to ensure they do not impose their own values on clients *(see Introduction and A.1.c.)*. Counselors respect the diversity of those they serve and address these issues with sensitivity and care. In all their professional interactions with others, counselors seek to promote each individual's best interests and to prevent harm to them.

Common Dilemmas and Conflicts

- Lack of awareness of personal values, beliefs, and attitudes can adversely impact the counseling relationship and process.
- Failure to anticipate the potential impact of one's statements and other behaviors can result in harm to clients, trainees, and research participants.
- It may be easy to forget that trainees and research participants deserve the same protections as clients.

Prevention and Positive Practice

✓ Before taking any actions, consider their potential impact on others; when an action might reasonably be expected to cause significant distress or harm, take extra time to determine the necessity of the action and strategies for minimizing harm.

✓ Engage in ongoing self-reflection to enhance awareness of your own values, attitudes, and beliefs and how they influence your counseling relationships.

✓ Be cautious about engaging in behaviors that are inconsistent with agreed-upon counseling goals.

✓ Always be respectful of clients' and others' diversity.

A.5. Roles and Relationships With Clients *(See F.3., F.10., G.3.)*

A.5.a. Current Clients

Sexual or romantic counselor–client interactions or relationships with current clients, their romantic partners, or their family members are prohibited.

A.5.b. Former Clients

Sexual or romantic counselor–client interactions or relationships with former clients, their romantic partners, or their family members are prohibited for a period of 5 years following the last professional contact. Counselors, before engaging in sexual or romantic interactions or relationships with clients, their romantic partners, or client family members after 5 years following the last professional contact, demonstrate forethought and document (in written form) whether the interactions or relationship can be viewed as exploitive in some way and/or whether there is still potential to harm the former client; in cases of potential exploitation and/or harm, the counselor avoids entering such an interaction or relationship.

Essential Elements

Because of the significant potential for harm to clients and the counseling relationship, sexual and romantic relationships are always prohibited with current clients or their significant others. Such relationships impair the objectivity of the counselor and are always seen as exploitative. Further, even after the counseling relationship has ended, entering into such sexual or romantic relationships should only be done with great caution. Such relationships may only occur after 5 years from the last professional contact and after careful consideration of the potential impact on the former client *(see A.1.a.)*. The counselor's motivations, the former client's vulnerability, and the likelihood of harm *(see A.4.a.)* must be considered, and the rationale for the decision should be documented. When any potential for exploitation or harm to the former client is present, this type of relationship should be avoided.

Common Dilemmas and Conflicts

- Counselors who fail to adequately attend to their own issues, needs, and self-care may be at risk for entering exploitative relationships with clients or former clients.

- Failure to respect and maintain appropriate boundaries in the counseling relationship may result in inappropriate sexual or romantic relationships.
- Placing one's own needs and interests over the client's or former client's may result in poor decisions about entering intimate relationships.
- Counselors experiencing relational problems, loneliness, or phase-of-life concerns may be at increased risk for engaging in inappropriate relationships with clients.

Prevention and Positive Practice

✓ Maintain healthy boundaries, engage in self-reflection, and practice ongoing self-care to ensure good decisions regarding relationships.

✓ Always consider how entering into a sexual or romantic relationship will affect the client, the counseling process and relationship, your objectivity, and others' view of the counseling profession.

✓ Maintain appropriate boundaries with clients' significant others, such as family members or partners.

✓ Realize that your commitment to each client's welfare and best interests does not end when the counseling relationship is completed.

✓ Keep in mind that a sexual or romantic relationship with a former client would preclude you from ever providing further counseling services to that person.

✓ Pay attention to warning signs such as fantasies about a client, extending sessions, or planning to meet a client in a nonprofessional setting; seek consultation from a trusted colleague or supervisor at once.

A.5.c. Nonprofessional Interactions or Relationships (Other Than Sexual or Romantic Interactions or Relationships)

Counselor–client nonprofessional relationships with clients, former clients, their romantic partners, or their family members should be avoided, except when the interaction is potentially beneficial to the client. *(See A.5.d.)*

A.5.d. Potentially Beneficial Interactions

When a counselor–client nonprofessional interaction with a client or former client may be potentially beneficial to the client or former client, the counselor must document in case records, prior to the interaction (when feasible), the rationale for such an interaction, the potential benefit, and anticipated consequences for the client or former client and other individuals significantly involved with the client or former client. Such interactions should be initiated with appropriate client consent. Where unintentional harm occurs to the client or former client, or to an individual significantly involved with the client or former client, due to the nonprofessional interaction, the counselor must show evidence of an attempt to remedy such harm. Examples of potentially beneficial interactions include, but are not limited to, attending a formal ceremony (e.g., a wedding/commitment ceremony or graduation); purchasing a service or product provided by a client or former client (excepting unrestricted bartering); hospital visits to an ill family member; mutual membership in a professional association, organization, or community. *(See A.5.c.)*

Essential Elements

While sexual and romantic behaviors and relationships with clients and their significant others should always be avoided, other nonprofessional interactions may be warranted when they are potentially beneficial to the client or former client. In some settings such as rural or remote locales, counselors may need to engage in multiple relationships with clients and former clients; they may interact routinely at school, church, and community events. At other times, counselors may participate appropriately in clients' important life events such as weddings or graduations. It is recommended that the rationale and anticipated benefits and potential consequences of such actions be documented in case records, and the counselor should only engage in the extra interaction after obtaining informed consent from the client. Should harm occur from these secondary relationships (e.g., embarrassment, anger about extra-counseling interactions, perceived reductions in the value of counseling), counselors must make every effort to minimize or remedy the harm. Before engaging in any voluntary nonprofessional interaction with clients, counselors carefully consider relevant state laws bearing on such interactions.

Common Dilemmas and Conflicts

- Counselors who do not consider the potential impact of secondary relationships on clients are at risk of having interactions that are potentially exploitative or harmful.
- A desire to avoid documentation and to keep secondary relationships secret places the counselor at risk for inappropriate relationships.
- Counselors who place their own needs over those of clients are more likely to enter potentially harmful relationships.
- Counselors living in rural locations are at greater risk for frequent nonprofessional interactions with clients.

Prevention and Positive Practice

✓ Only enter secondary relationships with clients and former clients when not clinically contraindicated and when the nature of the secondary relationship is not inconsistent with state laws or agency policies regarding nonprofessional contact with clients.

✓ Always use a thoughtful decision-making process when considering entering into another relationship with clients or former clients.

✓ When unsure about the appropriateness of certain relationships or types of interaction, consult with a supervisor or with experienced colleagues to assist in decision making.

✓ Document the rationale and decision-making process leading to all such decisions; include documentation of appropriate consultation.

A.5.e. Role Changes in the Professional Relationship

> When a counselor changes a role from the original or most recent contracted relationship, he or she obtains informed consent from the client and explains the right of the client to refuse services related to the change. Examples of role changes include

1. changing from individual to relationship or family counseling, or vice versa;
2. changing from a nonforensic evaluative role to a therapeutic role, or vice versa;
3. changing from a counselor to a researcher role (i.e., enlisting clients as research participants), or vice versa; and
4. changing from a counselor to a mediator role, or vice versa.

Clients must be fully informed of any anticipated consequences (e.g., financial, legal, personal, or therapeutic) of counselor role changes.

Essential Elements

One cannot always foresee the course of a counseling relationship at the outset; frequently, changes in professional relationship roles may occur. When such role changes are warranted and appropriate or legally required, obtain consent from the client *(see A.2.)*, appropriately update the counseling plan *(see A.1.c.)* and document *(see A.1.b.)* this change, and inform the client of any anticipated consequences. Examples include changing from individual to group counseling, or changing from counselor to mediator, forensic evaluator, or researcher. Counselors are vigilant to the possibility of role changes at the outset of each professional relationship and do their best to anticipate and respond to such changes before they interfere with the counseling relationship or create distress for the client.

Common Dilemmas and Conflicts

- Counselors who shift professional roles with clients without first engaging in informed consent risk harm to the client.
- Counselors who fail to consider the potential impact of role changes may jeopardize the counseling relationship.
- Counselors who change roles without careful consideration run the risk of engaging in incompatible multiple roles.

Prevention and Positive Practice

✓ Always consider the client's preferences and best interests when considering changing professional roles.

✓ Engage in an informed consent process with clients prior to changing roles, and be sure to fully discuss all anticipated risks, benefits, and implications.

✓ Be sure to provide adequate information to clients so they may make decisions about role shifts that are in their best interest; remember that the inherent power imbalance in counselor–client relationships may make a truly independent decision by the client difficult.

✓ When client needs go beyond the current role and you are unable to serve in the other capacity, referral to appropriately trained colleagues is needed.

✓ Never change roles for personal benefit; focus on how the new role will serve your client's best interest.

A.6. Roles and Relationships at Individual, Group, Institutional, and Societal Levels

A.6.a. Advocacy

When appropriate, counselors advocate at individual, group, institutional, and societal levels to examine potential barriers and obstacles that inhibit access and/or the growth and development of clients.

A.6.b. Confidentiality and Advocacy

Counselors obtain client consent prior to engaging in advocacy efforts on behalf of an identifiable client to improve the provision of services and to work toward removal of systemic barriers or obstacles that inhibit client access, growth, and development.

Essential Elements

Advocacy is an important role for counselors. Counselors work to remedy injustices that affect clients as well as the public at large and to promote equality and access to care *(see A.1.a.)*. Counselors are particularly vigilant to implicit and systemic barriers to client health and development. Advocacy efforts may occur on the individual, systemic, organizational, and societal level. Before counselors engage in advocacy efforts on behalf of a particular client, it is important to first obtain informed consent *(see A.2.a.)* to avoid violating the client's autonomy or confidentiality rights *(see B.1.a., B.1.b.)*.

Common Dilemmas and Conflicts

- Counselors who only see a limited professional role for themselves may neglect important advocacy opportunities that may be in keeping with the overarching values of the counseling profession.
- Counselors who are overzealous in their advocacy efforts may harm clients by violating their confidentiality rights.
- Ill-considered advocacy efforts may actually undermine a client's autonomy or may reflect the counselor's need to protect more than the client's need for advocacy.

Prevention and Positive Practice

✓ Counselors should honor their overarching obligations to society at large and consider advocacy an essential element of their professional roles.

✓ While use of client examples may prove compelling to decision makers, counselors should always obtain client informed consent before disclosing confidential information obtained in the counseling relationship.

✓ Advocacy activities should always be motivated by the welfare of those served by counselors and not by the counselor's personal agendas.

A.7. Multiple Clients

When a counselor agrees to provide counseling services to two or more persons who have a relationship, the counselor clarifies at the outset which person or persons are clients and the nature of the relationships the counselor will have with each involved person. If it becomes apparent that the counselor may be called upon to perform potentially conflicting roles, the counselor will clarify, adjust, or withdraw from roles appropriately. *(See A.8.a., B.4.)*

Essential Elements

At times counselors will be called upon to provide professional services to two or more persons who have an existing relationship; these may include family members, coworkers, or roommates. This may occur inadvertently or at clients' direct request. Simultaneous care for related clients may also occur when the counselor has needed clinical expertise and equally competent mental health professionals are not available. When serving multiple clients, counselors clarify all professional roles with each individual, and if potentially conflicting roles are likely or are discovered, counselors take appropriate actions to minimize the risk of harm to all involved *(see A.4.a, A.5.e.)*. The overarching goal of promoting each client's welfare *(see A.1.a.)* and attention to relevant laws or regulations should guide counselors' decisions in these situations.

Common Dilemmas and Conflicts

- Counselors who overlook the potential for impaired objectivity and conflicts of interest are especially vulnerable to difficulties with multiple clients.
- Failure to openly discuss all roles and relationships at the outset of counseling with multiple clients, or as soon as multiple roles become evident, may place each client at risk for harm.

Prevention and Positive Practice

✓ Carefully consider multiple client situations and seek consultation if unsure of the appropriateness of or need for them.

✓ Closely monitor the impact of serving multiple clients throughout the course of treatment to ensure that no adverse consequences occur.

✓ When concerns arise, openly discuss them with each client and take actions that are in each individual's best interests.

✓ Before counseling multiple clients, consider all reasonably available options and alternatives.

A.8. Group Work *(See B.4.a.)*

A.8.a. Screening

Counselors screen prospective group counseling/therapy participants. To the extent possible, counselors select members whose needs and goals are compatible with goals of the group, who will not impede the group process, and whose well-being will not be jeopardized by the group experience.

A.8.b. Protecting Clients

In a group setting, counselors take reasonable precautions to protect clients from physical, emotional, or psychological trauma.

Essential Elements

Group counseling and group psychotherapy are services that appropriately trained counselors provide. Selection of specific clients for group counseling requires specific competence in the area of group work *(see B.4.a.)*. Prior to accepting or placing clients in counseling groups, counselors should carefully screen them to ensure it is an appropriate placement, both for the individual client and for the other group participants. Counselors take active steps to ensure, to the extent possible, that clients are not harmed through their participation in the counseling or psychotherapy group *(see A.4.a.)*.

Common Dilemmas and Conflicts

- Counselors motivated by organizational or financial demands may overlook client needs and may inappropriately place clients in group counseling.
- Counselors may overlook the potential challenges and potential for harm group work may bring for some clients.

Prevention and Positive Practice

✓ Ensure that you are competent in this area before providing group counseling services.
✓ Carefully screen clients before including them in group work.
✓ Be sure informed consent addresses all potential risks and benefits that may come with the group format.
✓ Clearly articulate expectations for confidentiality and interpersonal behavior consistent with respect and safety.
✓ Take active precautions to minimize the risk of harm to group participants.

A.9. End-of-Life Care for Terminally Ill Clients

A.9.a. Quality of Care

Counselors strive to take measures that enable clients

1. to obtain high-quality end-of-life care for their physical, emotional, social, and spiritual needs;
2. to exercise the highest degree of self-determination possible;
3. to be given every opportunity possible to engage in informed decision making regarding their end-of-life care; and
4. to receive complete and adequate assessment regarding their ability to make competent, rational decisions on their own behalf from a mental health professional who is experienced in end-of-life care practice.

A.9.b. Counselor Competence, Choice, and Referral

Recognizing the personal, moral, and competence issues related to end-of-life decisions, counselors may choose to work or not work with terminally ill clients who wish to explore their end-of-life options. Counselors provide appropriate referral information to ensure that clients receive the necessary help.

A.9.c. Confidentiality

Counselors who provide services to terminally ill individuals who are considering hastening their own deaths have the option of breaking or not breaking confidentiality, depending on applicable laws and the specific circumstances of the situation and after seeking consultation or supervision from appropriate professional and legal parties. *(See B.5.c., B.7.c.)*

Essential Elements

When counseling clients with terminal illnesses, counselors take special care to maximize clients' quality of life by attending to their physical, emotional, social, and spiritual needs in a sensitive manner. Counselors respect terminally ill clients' autonomy and utilize informed consent to the extent possible *(see A.1.a., A.2.a.)*. When unsure of a client's ability to fully participate in informed consent, counselors should conduct a thorough and competent assessment of client capacity. Counselors who work with terminally ill clients ensure they have the necessary competence, ensure that values and personal beliefs do not interfere with clients' autonomous decision making, and, when needed, make referrals to other appropriately trained professionals. Counselors must follow applicable laws and should consult with knowledgeable colleagues or supervisors when unsure of how to proceed, especially when considering breaching confidentiality if clients are considering hastening the end of their life.

Common Dilemmas and Conflicts

- Counselors who lack the needed training and expertise may be ill prepared to work with clients facing end-of-life issues.
- Failure to attend to one's own values and beliefs may result in violating clients' autonomy and rights for self-determination.
- Lack of knowledge of applicable laws may result in violating both laws and clients' rights.

Prevention and Positive Practice

✓ Consider counseling work with clients facing end-of-life issues only after ensuring appropriate competence to practice in this area.
✓ Carefully monitor personal values and beliefs and prevent these from interfering with clients' right to self-determination.
✓ Be knowledgeable of appropriately trained colleagues; when a client's counseling needs exceed your competence or moral comfort, make referrals to competent colleagues.
✓ Take steps to promote each client's autonomous decision making and self-determination.
✓ Assess each client's ability to fully participate in the informed consent process and work to include their preferences in any way possible.

A.10. Fees and Bartering

A.10.a. Accepting Fees From Agency Clients

Counselors refuse a private fee or other remuneration for rendering services to persons who are entitled to such services through the counselor's employing agency or institution. The policies of a particular agency may make explicit provisions for agency clients to receive counseling services from members of its staff in private practice. In such instances, the clients must be informed of other options open to them should they seek private counseling services.

Essential Elements

Counselors always clarify fee arrangements prior to initiating the counseling relationship. Those who work for agencies or who provide counseling services to clients through agencies do not charge or accept fees from these clients when the agency does or would pay for the counseling services. Clients are always informed of their counseling treatment options in advance, including all fees and alternative sources for counseling in the community *(see A.1.a., A.2.a., A.2.b.)*.

Common Dilemmas and Conflicts

- Counselors who overlook the informed consent process are at risk of not informing clients of billing practices and counseling alternatives.
- Inattention to institutional policies and benefits for clients may result in counselors inappropriately billing clients.
- Counselors experiencing financial stress may be at risk of accepting inappropriate remuneration from clients.

Prevention and Positive Practice

✓ Always clarify financial arrangements from the outset of the counseling relationship and be familiar with all relevant institutional policies.
✓ Inform clients about all options reasonably available to them and the financial implications of selecting each.
✓ Never accept a fee from a client whose counseling is being paid for by an agency or institution.

A.10.b. Establishing Fees

In establishing fees for professional counseling services, counselors consider the financial status of clients and locality. In the event that the established fee structure is inappropriate for a client, counselors assist clients in attempting to find comparable services of acceptable cost.

A.10.c. Nonpayment of Fees

If counselors intend to use collection agencies or take legal measures to collect fees from clients who do not pay for services as agreed upon, they first inform clients of intended actions and offer clients the opportunity to make payment.

Essential Elements

While fee setting is an individual decision for each counselor, fees must be set with attention to both community norms and the welfare of clients and potential clients *(see A.1.a.)*. Fees should not make access to counseling services prohibitive for most members of a community. In those cases in which a client cannot afford the counselor's fees, the counselor should attempt to refer the client to a competent counselor or other mental health professional whose fees are more in line with the client's resources. When clients do not pay agreed-upon fees, counselors may use collection agencies or take legal action to collect the fees owed, but this should only be done after first informing the client of the intended actions and offering him or her the opportunity to make payment, such as with a payment plan over an agreed-upon period of time *(see A.2.a., A.2.b.)*. When an ongoing client's financial situation changes for the worse, counselors demonstrate care, flexibility, and a genuine effort to find a mutually acceptable revised financial arrangement with the client.

Common Dilemmas and Conflicts

- Counselors who do not address fees and financial arrangements in the informed consent process are at increased risk for difficulties in this area of practice.
- Counselors who use collection agencies or who take legal action to collect past-due fees without first attempting to work informally with the client to collect the fee often generate unnecessary conflict.
- Counselors who set fees that are inconsistent with prevailing community standards and clients' financial resources are likely to experience challenges in this area.

Prevention and Positive Practice

✓ Always address in the informed consent process all fees, payment expectations, and the potential for use of collection or legal procedures.

✓ Consider community standards and expectations as well as financial resources of local residents when setting fees.

✓ Maintain a list of competent mental health professionals and community agencies as referral resources in the event that clients are not able to afford your fees.

✓ When clients experience difficulty paying for counseling services—a common occurrence in difficult economic times—attempt a range of informal strategies for resolution prior to using collection agencies or taking legal action.

A.10.d. Bartering

> Counselors may barter only if the relationship is not exploitive or harmful and does not place the counselor in an unfair advantage, if the client requests it, and if such arrangements are an accepted practice among professionals in the community. Counselors consider the cultural implications of bartering and discuss relevant concerns with clients and document such agreements in a clear written contract.

Essential Elements

In some communities and in some circumstances, clients may not be able to afford to pay for counseling services but may be able to exchange goods (e.g., produce, firewood) or services (e.g., painting, landscaping) in exchange for counseling. This may be done as long as the client requests it, doing so is not exploitive of the client, and it is an acceptable practice in the local community. In addition, bartering is only acceptable if the bartering arrangement does not unfairly disadvantage the client. The use of barter should be addressed in the informed consent agreement *(see A.2.a., A.2.b.)*, and it should be documented in a written agreement. Finally, when considering a bartering arrangement, counselors should give attention to cultural issues and implications *(see A.2.c.)* and discuss these with clients before proceeding.

Common Dilemmas and Conflicts

- Failure to fully address the potential implications of bartering in the informed consent process may result in adverse impact for the client. When bartering becomes necessary for a client after the initial informed consent is obtained, revisit the informed consent process and discuss the implications of this new arrangement.
- Those overlooking cultural factors and implications may violate community expectations and standards.
- Counselors may inadvertently exploit clients when the value of bartered goods is difficult to determine.

Prevention and Positive Practice

✓ During economically difficult times, remain open to the possibility that barter arrangements will be the only alternative for some clients.
✓ Always reach an agreement on the value of all goods and services to be bartered in advance.
✓ Monitor the impact of barter on the counseling relationship over time and make adjustments as needed to ensure both parties feel fairly treated.
✓ Be sure the client's best interests are being met and that no exploitation is likely to occur.

A.10.e. Receiving Gifts

Counselors understand the challenges of accepting gifts from clients and recognize that in some cultures, small gifts are a token of respect and showing gratitude. When determining whether or not to accept a gift from clients, counselors take into account the therapeutic relationship, the monetary value of the gift, a client's motivation for giving the gift, and the counselor's motivation for wanting or declining the gift.

Essential Elements

At times clients may offer gifts to counselors as an expression of thanks for services provided or because of cultural norms and expectations around special events and holidays. Counselors must engage in careful thought and consideration prior to accepting or refusing gifts from clients. No absolute rules exist on this matter, and factors such as the nature of the therapeutic relationship, the cost or value of the gift, the meaning to and motivations of the client, and the counselor's motivations all must be considered. While violating a client's cultural beliefs or insulting them through rejection of a gift may be harmful, accepting gifts may also be harmful to clients if the gift is inappropriately motivated, inordinately expensive, or if the client may be exploited in the process.

Common Dilemmas and Conflicts

- Failure to consider client motivations, cultural expectations, and the meaning of the gift to the client may result in harm to the counseling relationship.
- Making decisions based on the counselor's own motivations and needs will likely result in exploitation or harm to the client.
- Counselors who uniformly refuse all gifts may cause as much damage to the counseling relationship as those who uncritically accept all gifts.

Prevention and Positive Practice

✓ Never suggest gift giving to a client.
✓ Explore the meaning of the gift to the client as well as the meaning of accepting or rejecting it when considering the most appropriate course of action.
✓ Be mindful of client vulnerabilities and your obligation to only take actions consistent with promoting client welfare.

A.11. Termination and Referral

A.11.a. Abandonment Prohibited

Counselors do not abandon or neglect clients in counseling. Counselors assist in making appropriate arrangements for the continuation of treatment, when necessary, during interruptions such as vacations, illness, and following termination.

A.11.b. Inability to Assist Clients

If counselors determine an inability to be of professional assistance to clients, they avoid entering or continuing counseling relationships. Counselors are knowledgeable about culturally and clinically appropriate referral resources and suggest these alternatives. If clients decline the suggested referrals, counselors should discontinue the relationship.

A.11.c. Appropriate Termination

Counselors terminate a counseling relationship when it becomes reasonably apparent that the client no longer needs assistance, is not likely to benefit, or is being harmed by continued counseling. Counselors may terminate counseling when in jeopardy of harm by the client, or another person with whom the client has a relationship, or when clients do not pay fees as agreed upon. Counselors provide pretermination counseling and recommend other service providers when necessary.

A.11.d. Appropriate Transfer of Services

When counselors transfer or refer clients to other practitioners, they ensure that appropriate clinical and administrative processes are completed and open communication is maintained with both clients and practitioners.

Essential Elements

All counseling relationships end, but not all end by mutual agreement or because treatment goals have been achieved. At times, a counselor may not be able to fulfill obligations or may need to withdraw from the professional relationship. When doing so, counselors should not abandon their clients; they should assess the clients' ongoing counseling needs and make referrals to other competent professionals. Counselors should terminate the counseling relationship when clients are not benefiting from treatment or when its continuation may result in harm *(see A.4.a., C.2.d.)*. Additionally, counselors may end the counseling relationship when threatened or harmed by a client or someone associated with the client. When treatment is transferred to another professional, counselors participate in this process and cooperate fully to help ensure a smooth transition to the new professional. When making referrals, counselors pay attention to clinical and cultural competence to ensure that clients' best interests are served *(see A.1.a.)*.

Common Dilemmas and Conflicts

- Counselors who place a significant emphasis on their financial needs may be at risk of continuing clients' care past when it should have appropriately been terminated.
- Counselors who are fearful of charges of abandonment may continue providing counseling services even when they are no longer effective or benefiting the client.
- Counselors who overestimate their counseling skills may avoid making referrals and provide services to clients outside of their expertise and competence.
- Counselors who become angry with a difficult client or a client who fails to pay fees may be more prone to an abrupt or otherwise unprofessional termination of services.

Prevention and Positive Practice

✓ To the extent possible, address termination issues in the informed consent process to include when, why, and how termination will most likely occur. As termination draws nearer, revisit this discussion as early as feasible and as often as needed to help clients anticipate and prepare for the ending.

✓ Be sensitive to feelings of abandonment by clients and, whenever possible, provide pretermination counseling to address these issues and to make any needed referral arrangements.

- ✓ Be knowledgeable of community resources so you can make needed referrals competently and appropriately.
- ✓ Make appropriate coverage arrangements with colleagues so that clients' counseling needs are appropriately addressed during periods of anticipated absence or unavailability.

A.12. Technology Applications

A.12.a. Benefits and Limitations

Counselors inform clients of the benefits and limitations of using information technology applications in the counseling process and in business/billing procedures. Such technologies include but are not limited to computer hardware and software, telephones, the World Wide Web, the Internet, online assessment instruments, and other communication devices.

A.12.b. Technology-Assisted Services

When providing technology-assisted distance counseling services, counselors determine that clients are intellectually, emotionally, and physically capable of using the application and that the application is appropriate for the needs of clients.

A.12.c. Inappropriate Services

When technology-assisted distance counseling services are deemed inappropriate by the counselor or client, counselors consider delivering services face to face.

A.12.d. Access

Counselors provide reasonable access to computer applications when providing technology-assisted distance counseling services.

A.12.e. Laws and Statutes

Counselors ensure that the use of technology does not violate the laws of any local, state, national, or international entity and observe all relevant statutes.

A.12.f. Assistance

Counselors seek business, legal, and technical assistance when using technology applications, particularly when the use of such applications crosses state or national boundaries.

Essential Elements

The use of a wide range of technologies may be of great assistance for billing and submitting claims, for communications between in-person counseling sessions, and for the provision of counseling services to clients who would not otherwise be able to access them (e.g., those in remote locales, those who are home bound).

However, technologies such as telephone, fax, computers, and the Internet must be used with caution. Before using them, counselors should fully address the benefits and limitations of these technologies with clients. Counselors ensure that the technology in question is appropriate for the particular client based on his or her intellectual, physical, and emotional needs and limitations. Counselors do not use technology inappropriately, such as when a client's needs clearly warrant the use of in-person counseling services. Counselors do not violate laws such as by offering services in jurisdictions where they are not licensed. Counselors consult with appropriate colleagues and experts when unsure if a specific technology is appropriate for use with a specific client or counseling issue.

Common Dilemmas and Conflicts

- Counselors who are enamored with the use of technology may be at risk for using it inappropriately.
- Failure to attend to relevant laws may result in providing services inappropriately.
- Counselors who do not first assess the appropriateness of using technology with individual clients may cause harm to clients.
- Counselors who fail to ensure that technology does not compromise confidentiality are at risk in this area.

Prevention and Positive Practice

✓ Ensure needed technical competence in the use of each technology.
✓ Understand the potential benefits, risks, and limitations of each technology before using it.
✓ Assess each client's appropriateness for the use of a technology, attending to physical, emotional, and technological limitations.
✓ Be knowledgeable of laws and statutes relevant to providing counseling services using various technologies.
✓ Always consult with technological, legal, and counseling experts to ensure the appropriate use and application of technologies in counseling.

A.12.g. Technology and Informed Consent

As part of the process of establishing informed consent, counselors do the following:

1. Address issues related to the difficulty of maintaining the confidentiality of electronically transmitted communications.
2. Inform clients of all colleagues, supervisors, and employees, such as Information Technology (IT) administrators, who might have authorized or unauthorized access to electronic transmissions.
3. Urge clients to be aware of all authorized or unauthorized users including family members and fellow employees who have access to any technology clients may use in the counseling process.
4. Inform clients of pertinent legal rights and limitations governing the practice of a profession over state lines or international boundaries.

5. Use encrypted Web sites and e-mail communications to help ensure confidentiality when possible.
6. When the use of encryption is not possible, counselors notify clients of this fact and limit electronic transmissions to general communications that are not client specific.
7. Inform clients if and for how long archival storage of transaction records is maintained.
8. Discuss the possibility of technology failure and alternative methods of service delivery.
9. Inform clients of emergency procedures, such as calling 911 or a local crisis hotline, when the counselor is not available.
10. Discuss time zone differences, local customs, and cultural or language differences that might impact service delivery.
11. Inform clients when technology-assisted distance counseling services are not covered by insurance. *(See A.2.)*

Essential Elements

While the use of technology has many potential benefits, it brings with it a number of potential risks and limitations. Elements of risk attached to the use of technology should be fully discussed with clients as part of the informed consent agreement *(see A.2.a., A.2.b.)*. All threats and limits to confidentiality that come with the use of technology and the risks of access by others to counseling communications shared via technology should be discussed with clients. Online communications should be protected with encryption when possible, and when not, clients should be informed of this fact and communications should not include specific client information. Counselors should collaborate with clients to make plans for potential technology failures and for emergencies as part of the informed consent agreement. All other factors that may affect the viability and use of technology in counseling should be discussed, and counselors should inform clients if their insurance does not cover services provided through electronic means prior to offering the service.

Common Dilemmas and Conflicts

- Counselors lacking technological savvy and expertise are at risk for misusing these technologies to the detriment of clients.
- Counselors who assume that communications with clients through various technologies will be confidential place clients' privacy at great risk.
- Failure to fully address the use of technologies through the informed consent process may result in adverse outcomes for the client and the counseling relationship.

Prevention and Positive Practice

✓ Obtain the needed training to use various technologies appropriately in counseling.

✓ Educate clients about the use of technologies in counseling and sensitize them to precautions they should take to protect their confidentiality.

✓ Address all potential benefits and limitations of the use of technology in counseling at the outset.

✓ Make advance arrangements for technologic failures, emergency situations, and record storage.
✓ Confirm insurance coverage of counseling services provided via technologies prior to offering these services.

A.12.h. Sites on the World Wide Web

Counselors maintaining sites on the World Wide Web (the Internet) do the following:

1. Regularly check that electronic links are working and professionally appropriate.
2. Establish ways clients can contact the counselor in case of technology failure.
3. Provide electronic links to relevant state licensure and professional certification boards to protect consumer rights and facilitate addressing ethical concerns.
4. Establish a method for verifying client identity.
5. Obtain the written consent of the legal guardian or other authorized legal representative prior to rendering services in the event the client is a minor child, an adult who is legally incompetent, or an adult incapable of giving informed consent.
6. Strive to provide a site that is accessible to persons with disabilities
7. Strive to provide translation capabilities for clients who have a different primary language while also addressing the imperfect nature of such translations.
8. Assist clients in determining the validity and reliability of information found on the World Wide Web and other technology applications.

Essential Elements

Professional Web sites are widely used by counselors for providing important information to the public, for marketing one's counseling practice, and for allowing clients access to counseling services and important information. Counselors who offer Web sites have a responsibility to ensure that all content is current and accurate, functional links are provided to relevant licensure and professional certification boards, other means of contacting the counselor are provided should there be a technology failure, the site is accessible to individuals with disabilities, and translation capabilities are provided for clients not fluent in the language of the material posted on the Web site. Additionally, counselors with Web sites establish means for verifying the identity of individuals accessing counseling services via one's Web site and for obtaining their informed consent prior to providing the counseling services. Counselors ensure that their Web sites clearly describe how to appropriately use the information posted there. They do not imply or state that the information on the Web site is equivalent to professional advice or the counseling relationship.

Common Dilemmas and Conflicts

- Failure to attend to accessibility issues during Web site development may render one's Web site inaccessible to many clients.

- Failure to update content and ensure the functionality and accuracy of links on one's Web site can result in a poor experience for clients.
- Failure to provide clients with alternative means of contacting you may result in abandonment issues should technology failures occur.

Prevention and Positive Practice

✓ Always maintain responsibility for the content and functioning of your Web site, checking it regularly to ensure its appropriate functioning.

✓ Consult with accessibility experts when designing your Web site to ensure reasonable access by consumers regardless of disability, language, or other relevant factors.

✓ Establish informed consent, identity verification, and emergency contact procedures prior to providing services via a Web site or the Internet.

✓ Inform clients about the appropriate use of Web sites and the Internet, how to evaluate information provided there, and how to access licensure boards and other agencies should they have ethics concerns.

Section B

Confidentiality, Privileged Communication, and Privacy

Introduction

Counselors recognize that trust is a cornerstone of the counseling relationship. Counselors aspire to earn the trust of clients by creating an ongoing partnership, establishing and upholding appropriate boundaries, and maintaining confidentiality. Counselors communicate the parameters of confidentiality in a culturally competent manner.

Essential Elements

It all comes down to trust. Counselors appreciate the fact that the quality and efficacy of any professional relationship will hinge on the counselor's capacity to earn clients' trust. There are a variety of ways to communicate respect and inspire trust. These include creating an atmosphere of collaboration, establishing and maintaining appropriate and workable boundaries, avoiding intrusions on privacy, and carefully—even assiduously—maintaining confidentiality. Finally, counselors are ethically obligated to clearly and effectively help clients appreciate all limits to confidentiality in language they can understand and to use an approach that respects clients' cultural experiences and identities.

B.1. Respecting Client Rights

B.1.a. Multicultural/Diversity Considerations

Counselors maintain awareness and sensitivity regarding cultural meanings of confidentiality and privacy. Counselors respect differing views toward disclosure of information. Counselors hold ongoing discussions with clients as to how, when, and with whom information is to be shared.

B.1.b. Respect for Privacy

Counselors respect client rights to privacy. Counselors solicit private information from clients only when it is beneficial to the counseling process.

B.1.c. Respect for Confidentiality

Counselors do not share confidential information without client consent or without sound legal or ethical justification.

B.1.d. Explanation of Limitations

At initiation and throughout the counseling process, counselors inform clients of the limitations of confidentiality and seek to identify foreseeable situations in which confidentiality must be breached. *(See A.2.b.)*

Essential Elements

Clients have a right to determine the time, circumstances, and content of their disclosures; they enjoy a basic right to privacy. To respect clients' right to privacy, counselors must avoid soliciting private information that is not directly germane to the counseling process and the client's explicit goals. Counselors further protect clients' privacy by adamantly refusing to disclose confidential information about a client without the client's full consent or without another compelling legal/ethical justification. Respect for confidentiality is a nearly sacred obligation among counselors, and it is essential to the development of trust and the success of counseling relationships. During the informed consent process *(see A.2.)* and throughout the counseling relationship, counselors consider each client's cultural understanding of personal privacy, confidentiality, and disclosure. Counselors remain sensitive to the wide variations in culture-based preferences for sharing information with community or family members and adjust their procedures to reflect each client's informed preferences. Finally, counselors offer a detailed description—both verbally and in writing—of the likely occasions in which confidentiality would be breached. Counselors help clients to understand that confidentiality is not absolute and, to the extent possible, describe those limits and exceptions to confidentiality that the counselor can reasonably predict.

Common Dilemmas and Conflicts

- Assuming that all clients share a Western perspective on the concepts of privacy and disclosure may lead to misunderstanding and conflict.
- Counselors who either violate confidentiality without consent or refuse to disclose information when a client requests such a disclosure may be in violation of this section.
- Loss of focus on the client's primary goals, poor boundaries, or simple curiosity may lead a counselor to solicit irrelevant information and violate a client's privacy.
- Counselors who fail to explain the limits or exceptions to confidentiality in language clients can understand may have problems in this area.

Prevention and Positive Practice

- ✓ Respect and actively protect each client's right to privacy and confidentiality.
- ✓ Remember that confidentiality is both an ethical and—in many jurisdictions—a legal obligation.
- ✓ Carefully avoid questions and inquiries about private matters that have no relevance to the goals of counseling.
- ✓ Explore the culturally based meaning and importance that each client may attach to matters such as personal privacy and disclosure to family or other members of the cultural community.
- ✓ Develop ironclad policies for avoiding disclosure of client information unless disclosure is clearly authorized or mandated.
- ✓ Discuss the limitations to confidentiality with clients—both at the outset of counseling and throughout the relationship—and work to ensure that they understand the circumstances that would trigger a disclosure.
- ✓ Always remember that confidentiality belongs to the client and that the client may waive his or her right to confidentiality.
- ✓ Before advocating for a client *(see A.6.b.)*, first obtain client consent.

B.2. Exceptions

B.2.a. Danger and Legal Requirements

> The general requirement that counselors keep information confidential does not apply when disclosure is required to protect clients or identified others from serious and foreseeable harm or when legal requirements demand that confidential information must be revealed. Counselors consult with other professionals when in doubt as to the validity of an exception. Additional considerations apply when addressing end-of-life issues. *(See A.9.c.)*

Essential Elements

At times, counselors must breach confidentiality for the purpose of protecting clients or other persons from harm. Some of the most common limits to confidentiality bearing on the issue of danger or risk of harm include (a) when a client is suicidal and poses a danger to him- or herself, (b) when a client threatens harm to an identifiable individual or group, or (c) when a counselor suspects abuse or neglect of a child or other dependent person. Of course, it is essential that counselors elicit informed consent from clients at the outset of the counseling relationship so that clients understand these limitations to confidentiality up front *(see A.2., B.1.d.)*. Further, counselors must be thoroughly familiar with state and federal laws regarding the duty to warn, the duty to protect, and the duty to report abuse of children and other vulnerable persons.

Common Dilemmas and Conflicts

- Counselors who lack familiarity with key state and federal laws bearing on duty to warn and protect clients and others may be at risk in this area.

- Failure to routinely assess and document threat level in clients who have been suicidal or threatening to others may suggest professional negligence.
- Counselors who lack experience or competence in conducting risk assessments may miss key warning signs or overrespond when threat level is low.

Prevention and Positive Practice

✓ Accept the obligation to intervene when a client poses a real threat to self or to identifiable others.
✓ At times, protecting the client and others may involve providing more intensive treatment to protect the client from acting on impulse; at other times, fulfilling this obligation may necessitate a breach of confidentiality and contact with authorities.
✓ Know your own jurisdiction's legal requirements when it comes to exceptions to confidentiality.
✓ Clearly inform clients of the limits of confidentiality in these circumstances in advance.
✓ Routinely seek consultation with knowledgeable colleagues when deciding whether to violate confidentiality for the purpose of protecting someone from harm.
✓ When a terminally ill client is considering hastening his or her own death, review state and federal guidelines, review ethical considerations *(see A.9.c.)*, and seek consultation.

B.2.b. Contagious, Life-Threatening Diseases

> When clients disclose that they have a disease commonly known to be both communicable and life threatening, counselors may be justified in disclosing information to identifiable third parties, if they are known to be at demonstrable and high risk of contracting the disease. Prior to making a disclosure, counselors confirm that there is such a diagnosis and assess the intent of clients to inform the third parties about their disease or to engage in any behaviors that may be harmful to an identifiable third party.

Essential Elements

Counselors should be prepared when a client discloses being HIV positive or when a client acknowledges having a similar life-threatening and contagious disease. When this information comes to light, the *ACA Code of Ethics* does not require disclosure but emphasizes that a counselor *may* breach confidentiality. Before deciding whether to disclose this information to identifiable third parties who may be at risk of infection, counselors must consider several key factors. First, what do state laws have to say about confidentiality and HIV status? Many state laws prohibit counselors from disclosing any information relevant to a client's health status without consent. Second, can the counselor confirm the presence of a life-threatening disease? Third, is the client willing to take voluntary steps to protect others from harm (e.g., practice safe sex, warn potential sexual partners of his or her status)? Finally, is there a clearly identifiable person who is likely to be harmed or infected should the counselor not breach confidentiality?

Common Dilemmas and Conflicts

- Counselors who ignore state laws relating to appropriate circumstances for breaching confidentiality either may fail to take mandated action to warn or protect or may do so when such disclosures are clearly illegal.
- Counselors who disclose a client's disease status without first making an effort to confirm the diagnosis or elicit agreement from the client to protect others from infection are at risk of an ethical or legal violation in this area.

Prevention and Positive Practice

✓ Take a client's disclosure of a life-threatening and communicable disease seriously.
✓ Make an effort to secure confirmation of the client's medical status.
✓ Carefully explore state laws bearing on HIV and the limits of confidentiality.
✓ Be careful not to allow personal values to influence decisions about when to make a disclosure in the case of an HIV-positive client *(see A.4.b.).*
✓ Thoroughly explore the client's willingness to warn and to protect prospective sexual partners from infection.
✓ Should a client be unwilling or unable to guarantee such proactive efforts to protect others, seek expert consultation before deciding whether it is appropriate to breach confidentiality and attempt to warn a person who is clearly identifiable and very likely at great risk of infection.

B.2.c. Court-Ordered Disclosure

When subpoenaed to release confidential or privileged information without a client's permission, counselors obtain written, informed consent from the client or take steps to prohibit the disclosure or have it limited as narrowly as possible due to potential harm to the client or counseling relationship.

B.2.d. Minimal Disclosure

To the extent possible, clients are informed before confidential information is disclosed and are involved in the disclosure decision-making process. When circumstances require the disclosure of confidential information, only essential information is revealed.

Essential Elements

At times, a counselor may be subpoenaed by an attorney or ordered by a judge to both release confidential records and testify in court. Like all citizens, counselors are obligated to respect the laws in the jurisdictions in which they practice. In some circumstances, counselors cannot be forced to testify or release confidential records, such as when communication with a client is considered privileged under state or federal statutes, or when a counselor is subpoenaed in a civil proceeding (e.g., divorce, disability, child custody) that would not qualify as an exception to privileged communication. Whatever the circumstances of a court-ordered disclosure, counselors attempt to obtain full written consent *(see A.2.)* from clients before agreeing to release any records or make any disclosure. To serve the client's best interests, protect the client from harm, and preserve the counseling relationship, counselors should keep the client informed and involved in the process of responding to a formal request for disclosure. If a counselor must testify—with or without a client's consent—then the counselor works to limit the amount of information disclosed to only the most essential information; counselors work diligently to prevent irrelevant disclosures and unnecessary intrusions on privacy.

Common Dilemmas and Conflicts

- Counselors who are not thoroughly familiar with relevant state and federal statutes governing confidentiality and privileged communication in their jurisdictions will be at risk in this area.
- Counselors who refuse to comply with lawful court orders requiring disclosure of confidential information may place themselves in jeopardy legally and ethically.
- Counselors who fail to carefully screen subpoenas or other requests for disclosure and those who fail to limit information to only what is relevant and essential may be at risk of violating a client's confidentiality.

Prevention and Positive Practice

✓ Before responding to a subpoena or court order, seek consultation from experienced colleagues, state counseling associations, your state licensing board, and, when the circumstances are complicated or involve high conflict, your attorney.

✓ Before responding to a subpoena or court order, contact your client and carefully explain the request, your legal obligations, and any options the client has related to your response.

✓ Always attempt to elicit informed consent from a client before releasing any record or making any statement in court.

✓ Make your client an active participant in determining the most appropriate response to a subpoena or court order.

✓ Periodically review state and federal laws bearing on court-ordered disclosures and privileged communication.

✓ At all times, limit the extent and nature of your disclosure to prevent unnecessary breaches of confidentiality and violations of privacy.

B.3. Information Shared With Others

B.3.a. Subordinates

Counselors make every effort to ensure that privacy and confidentiality of clients are maintained by subordinates, including employees, supervisees, students, clerical assistants, and volunteers. *(See F.1.c.)*

Essential Elements

Whenever counselors supervise or employ others, they provide thorough and ongoing training and oversight to ensure that subordinates are vigilant about protecting client privacy and confidentiality. *Subordinates* encompass employees, supervisees, students, office staff, and volunteers. Counselors are always responsible—ethically and legally—for the behavior of their subordinates.

Common Dilemmas and Conflicts

- Counselors who are too busy or who supervise too many subordinates may be at risk in this area.
- Those who assume subordinates understand the concepts of privacy and confidentiality and how to protect them may be unpleasantly surprised.
- Failing to provide adequate ongoing training and supervision of subordinates in this area is a recipe for conflict.

Prevention and Positive Practice

✓ Carefully train and oversee new subordinates and supervisees to ensure that client privacy and confidentiality are protected.

✓ Never assume that trainees, employees, supervisees, or others understand the significance of confidentiality and how to safeguard it.

✓ Carefully monitor office procedures to detect any compromises in this area early.

✓ Review policies and provide training with subordinates on an ongoing basis to ensure their compliance.

B.3.b. Treatment Teams

> When client treatment involves a continued review or participation by a treatment team, the client will be informed of the team's existence and composition, information being shared, and the purposes of sharing such information.

Essential Elements

Many clients may benefit greatly from a team treatment approach. However, because clients may assume that the counselor does not share counseling information with others, it is essential to inform clients that the treatment team exists, who the members are, and what information team members will have access to. Counselors should seek client consent for such an arrangement and should clearly inform clients of the rationale for a team treatment approach. This subsection is equally relevant to group or team supervision arrangements; clients must be informed when others will have access to records or otherwise consult with the counselor about the client's care. If a client refuses consent for a multidisciplinary team or supervision team to have access to his or her confidential record, then the counselor must refrain from engaging these groups; if such modalities are required in an organization, then the client must be given the opportunity not to participate in counseling.

Common Dilemmas and Conflicts

- It may be easy to overlook the threat to a client's privacy and confidentiality when the client is unaware of who has access to confidential information.

- Counselors who assume that a client would endorse a team treatment approach or case consultation may be at risk in this area.

Prevention and Positive Practice

✓ Always provide clear and updated information regarding the identities of treatment team members, the purpose for a team approach, and the information the team will have access to.

✓ Always inform clients up front about ongoing consultation or treatment team arrangements.

✓ Attempt to elicit collaboration from clients by discussing the rationale for teamwork and consultation.

B.3.c. Confidential Settings

Counselors discuss confidential information only in settings in which they can reasonably ensure client privacy.

Essential Elements

It is frequently useful to discuss a client with a colleague or to seek consultation for a challenging case. In addition to the obligation to protect the client's confidentiality in these instances *(see B.1.c.)*, it is also essential to avoid such discussions in a public setting that may jeopardize client privacy *(see B.1.b.)*. It is equally important to avoid professional conversations with clients in nonprivate settings, such as during a chance encounter in the community.

Common Dilemmas and Conflicts

- Counselors are human. It can be terribly tempting to share fascinating case material with another professional in a social or public setting.
- Failure to think carefully about context and privacy can easily lead to unintentional violations of client confidentiality.

Prevention and Positive Practice

✓ In small communities, discuss in advance with clients your rationale for not discussing private matters during chance encounters.

✓ Remain vigilant to setting and context and refuse to discuss client material with a colleague or consultant when privacy cannot be guaranteed.

B.3.d. Third-Party Payers

Counselors disclose information to third-party payers only when clients have authorized such disclosure.

B.3.e. Transmitting Confidential Information

Counselors take precautions to ensure the confidentiality of information transmitted through the use of computers, electronic mail, facsimile machines, telephones, voicemail, answering machines, and other electronic or computer technology. *(See A.12.g.)*

Essential Elements

Many clients will elect to use a health insurance benefit to help cover the cost of professional counseling. Insurance companies and other third-party payers will often require documentation of counseling services such as diagnoses, type of service rendered, and the specific dates of counseling sessions. Counselors should never disclose this information to a third party without explicit authorization from the client. Even with consent, the counselor should disclose only the information considered essential for processing reimbursement *(see B.2.d.)* and only in a manner that complies with state and federal laws bearing on health insurance coverage. Further, counselors are particularly careful to protect the confidentiality of any client information transmitted electronically *(see A.12.g.)*.

Common Dilemmas and Conflicts

- When a client elects to seek reimbursement from an insurance company or other entity, a counselor may erroneously assume that the client consents to the release of information to that entity.
- Counselors who are unfamiliar with statutes governing clients' rights and limits to third-party disclosures may be at risk in this area.
- Counselors accustomed to transmitting confidential client information using electronic technology may become complacent or inattentive about risks to privacy.

Prevention and Positive Practice

✓ Always secure written client authorization before disclosing any information about counseling services to an insurance company or other third party.

✓ When making such a disclosure, provide only the minimum information required for reimbursement and prevent unnecessary violations of privacy.

✓ Study the provisions of the federal Health Insurance Portability and Accountability Act of 1996 (HIPAA; http://aspe.hhs.gov/admnsimp/pl104191.htm), and carefully adhere to HIPAA's strict provisions for sharing information with insurance providers.

✓ Make every effort to ensure that client information transmitted through electronic media is secure and off-limits to unauthorized persons; follow HIPAA rules governing such transmission.

B.3.f. Deceased Clients

Counselors protect the confidentiality of deceased clients, consistent with legal requirements and agency or setting policies.

Essential Elements

When a client dies, counselors remain committed to protecting the deceased person's privacy and confidentiality. The obligation to offer such protection remains in perpetuity. At times, legal requirements and agency policies extend or modify this duty, and counselors must remain aware of the relevant statutes governing professional obligations to deceased clients in their jurisdiction.

Common Dilemmas and Conflicts

- Counselors who overlook the obligation to protect privacy and confidentiality even after a client's death may run afoul of both ethical and legal guidelines.
- Counselors who either refuse to provide information to a deceased client's legal custodian when this is required by law, or who too quickly release information when not compelled by an appropriate legal authority, may be at risk in this area.
- A counselor who is emotionally affected by a client's death may be more inclined to make an unethical disclosure.

Prevention and Positive Practice

✓ Remember that your obligation to protect a client's confidentiality nearly always extends after his or her death.
✓ Become familiar with the legal requirements in your jurisdictions and the policies of your organization or agency bearing on the privacy and confidentiality of deceased clients.
✓ When a client is terminally ill or death is imminent, attempt to obtain clear consent and document a plan—in concert with relevant statutes—for protecting confidentiality and managing client records.

B.4. Groups and Families

B.4.a. Group Work

In group work, counselors clearly explain the importance and parameters of confidentiality for the specific group being entered.

B.4.b. Couples and Family Counseling

In couples and family counseling, counselors clearly define who is considered "the client" and discuss expectations and limitations of confidentiality. Counselors seek agreement and document in writing such agreement among all involved parties having capacity to give consent concerning each individual's right to confidentiality and any obligation to preserve the confidentiality of information known.

Essential Elements

In individual counselor–client relationships, confidentiality is exclusively the counselor's responsibility. But the presence of other people in group work and in couples and family counseling can quickly complicate issues of privacy and confidentiality. Counselors practicing group, couples, and family modalities must take extra time to carefully inform all members of the group or client system of the significant limits to confidentiality. In essence, a counselor can never guarantee confidentiality when more than one client is involved; group or family members may reveal information to others without the consent of either the counselor or other members of the system. In group work and in couples and family counseling, counselors clarify the nature of their relationship to each member of the system and establish clear agreement about matters such as exceptions to confidentiality, the handling of individual disclosures to the counselor, and the creation and release of records based on services involving multiple clients.

Common Dilemmas and Conflicts

- When counselors neglect to thoroughly inform clients that another person (group or family member) may violate their confidentiality, clients may be more inclined to feel harmed if such a violation occurs.
- Counselors who provide more than one mode of counseling for a client simultaneously (e.g., individual, group, couples) increase the risk of problems related to multiple roles *(see A.5.)* and inadvertent violations of confidentiality.
- Counselors who fail to establish separate records for each individual in one of these multiple-client modalities will have greater difficulty ensuring confidentiality when records are later requested.

Prevention and Positive Practice

✓ Clearly inform each participant in group, couples, or family counseling of the limits of confidentiality, discuss these limitations and obtain written consent before providing these services.

✓ Clearly communicate the need for confidentiality to all participants and firmly establish confidentiality as a group or family system norm.

✓ Clearly inform clients that you cannot enforce a ban on violations of confidentiality even though this is a firm expectation in group, couples, and family counseling.

✓ When a client receives more than one form of counseling in an agency or practice, establish and communicate transparent guidelines regarding the sharing of client information between counselors.

✓ Make sure that records for each client are kept separate, and avoid referring to other group members in clients' records.

✓ Only provide those parts of a record germane to the requesting client, and do not release any confidential information related to another member of a group or system without his or her consent.

✓ Clearly communicate your policy about keeping, or not keeping, secrets disclosed by group, couple, or family members in advance of starting counseling.

B.5. Clients Lacking Capacity to Give Informed Consent

B.5.a. Responsibility to Clients

When counseling minor clients or adult clients who lack the capacity to give voluntary, informed consent, counselors protect the confidentiality of information received in the counseling relationship as specified by federal and state laws, written policies, and applicable ethical standards.

B.5.b. Responsibility to Parents and Legal Guardians

Counselors inform parents and legal guardians about the role of counselors and the confidential nature of the counseling relationship. Counselors are sensitive to the cultural diversity of families and respect the inherent rights and responsibilities of parents/guardians over the welfare of their children/charges according to law. Counselors work to establish, as appropriate, collaborative relationships with parents/guardians to best serve clients.

B.5.c. Release of Confidential Information

When counseling minor clients or adult clients who lack the capacity to give voluntary consent to release confidential information, counselors seek permission from an appropriate third party to disclose information. In such instances, counselors inform clients consistent with their level of understanding and take culturally appropriate measures to safeguard client confidentiality.

Essential Elements

Counselors who work with minors or with adults who are unable to provide voluntary or legal informed consent must be particularly vigilant to protecting confidentiality while balancing laws and statutes; laws regarding minors vary widely among jurisdictions. Because confidentiality is essential to the counseling process, and because some states ensure confidentiality for minors seeking certain types of mental health and medical care, counselors are thoroughly versed in laws bearing on the rights of minors, the rights of legal guardians, and those circumstances in which disclosure to a parent or guardian is required by law. Counselors clearly communicate role expectations for everyone involved at the outset of counseling to prevent misunderstanding, and they work collaboratively with parents and guardians—when legally appropriate—to provide care that will serve the client's best interests. Finally, counselors are mindful of the ways that culture may influence views about confidentiality. When working with children, adult clients who lack the capacity to provide consent, and legal guardians, counselors are especially careful to respect cultural values and worldviews. For instance, counselors are sensitive to collectivist perspectives that minimize the salience of individual confidentiality.

Common Dilemmas and Conflicts

- In their efforts to safeguard confidentiality, counselors may fail to communicate appropriately and collaboratively with parents and legal guardians.
- When a counselor is unfamiliar with the laws bearing on the rights of minors and adults who cannot provide legal consent, the risk of ethical and legal difficulty in this area escalates.
- Counselors who are too quick to provide client information when pressed by parents or other adults may inadvertently violate confidentiality in some circumstances.

Prevention and Positive Practice

- ✓ Be careful to clearly communicate the roles and rights—including the right to confidentiality—of everyone involved when counseling a minor client or an adult who cannot provide legal consent.
- ✓ Be fully familiar with the state and federal statutes relative to provision of counseling to minors in your jurisdiction.
- ✓ When pressed for information from a parent or guardian, first explore your legal and ethical responsibilities to all parties involved and consider seeking consultation from a colleague with experience in this area.
- ✓ Appreciate the influence of culture on perceptions of children's rights, autonomy in decision making, and the significance of family and community in caring for minors and disabled adults.
- ✓ Always provide informed consent regarding the client's rights and your obligations to prevent misunderstanding about confidentiality.

B.6. Records

B.6.a. Confidentiality of Records

> Counselors ensure that records are kept in a secure location and that only authorized persons have access to records.

Essential Elements

Counselors remain mindful of the fact that clients' rights to confidentiality extend to any record (e.g., case notes, electronic recordings, billing statements) of their care. To keep records confidential, counselors put stringent measures in place that limit access to records and ensure that they are stored in a safe location—typically in a professional office with multiple levels of security.

Common Dilemmas and Conflicts

- Over time, counselors may become complacent about record security.
- Counselors who make it a practice to leave client records out in their offices or take records home are at greater risk in this area.
- Failing to train office staff in record security procedures heightens the risk of violations to client confidentiality.

Prevention and Positive Practice

- ✓ Carefully review state laws bearing on record maintenance and storage in your jurisdiction.
- ✓ Carefully review federal guidelines bearing on record maintenance, such as the Health Insurance Portability and Accountability Act (HIPAA; http://aspe.hhs.gov/admnsimp/pl104191.htm).
- ✓ Establish office or agency policies regarding record maintenance and ensure that all staff, employees, and trainees abide by them.
- ✓ Maintain professionalism by keeping all written and electronic client records stored securely, usually in a locked office and in a locked file cabinet.
- ✓ Avoid taking client records out of the office.

B.6.b. Permission to Record

Counselors obtain permission from clients prior to recording sessions through electronic or other means.

B.6.c. Permission to Observe

Counselors obtain permission from clients prior to observing counseling sessions, reviewing session transcripts, or viewing recordings of sessions with supervisors, faculty, peers, or others within the training environment.

Essential Elements

Counselors never make any recording of a client (e.g., audio, video, digital, photographic) without first obtaining clear written permission. In addition, counselors always obtain permission from clients before allowing others (e.g., colleagues, consultants, supervisors) to observe counseling sessions or review recordings or other records of counseling sessions. Similarly, counselors verify that other counselors' clients have granted permission before serving as an observer, consultant, or supervisor themselves. Permitting observation of counseling sessions or recording clients should only be done to further the best interests of the client.

Common Dilemmas and Conflicts

- Just because session recording or supervision is intended to benefit the client, counselors are not absolved of the duty to obtain written permission first.
- Counselors working under supervision, those participating in consultation groups, or those employed by an agency may overlook the requirement to obtain permission before allowing others to observe their work or review client records.

Prevention and Positive Practice

✓ If the recording of sessions or the use of consultants or supervisors is part of your standard practice, always obtain the client's written permission for these activities at the outset of a counseling relationship.

✓ Never make a recording of a counseling session without explicit permission from the client.

✓ Always remain sensitive to clients' reactions to recordings or observations; consider discontinuing these practices if they are distressing to clients.

✓ Counselors working in training environments must remember that recording, observation, and record review must be cleared in advance with every client individually; avoid assuming that consent is implicit.

B.6.d. Client Access

Counselors provide reasonable access to records and copies of records when requested by competent clients. Counselors limit the access of clients to their records, or portions of their records, only when there is compelling evidence that such access would cause harm to the client. Counselors document the request of clients and the rationale for withholding some or all of the record in the files of clients. In situations involving multiple clients, counselors provide individual clients with only those parts of records that relate directly to them and do not include confidential information related to any other client.

B.6.e. Assistance With Records

When clients request access to their records, counselors provide assistance and consultation in interpreting counseling records.

B.6.f. Disclosure or Transfer

Unless exceptions to confidentiality exist, counselors obtain written permission from clients to disclose or transfer records to legitimate third parties. Steps are taken to ensure that receivers of counseling records are sensitive to their confidential nature. *(See A.3., E.4.)*

Essential Elements

Clients have a right to access and review their records. When competent clients make a request to see their records, counselors should cooperate with the request; they should provide the consultation and interpretation required for the client to fully understand and benefit from the record review. In some instances, a counselor may determine that viewing some or all of the record may actually harm a client *(see A.4.a.)*. In this case, the counselor may restrict access to the record, but in so doing should carefully document the rationale and work with the client to reduce misunderstanding or conflict. Before releasing a record or allowing a client to review a record, first ensure that information about any other client—such as in group or family counseling—is removed. Finally, when releasing a record to an appropriate third party, based on a client's valid written consent or a clear exception to confidentiality, clearly communicate the confidential nature of the record.

Common Dilemmas and Conflicts

- Counselors who are authoritarian or overly paternalistic may refuse to make clients' records available to them for review when they so request and be at risk for violating a client's right in this area.
- Counselors who automatically provide the entire record for a client to review—without considering whether some portions could cause harm to the client—may inadvertently cause harm to the client.
- Disclosing or transferring a record at a client's request does not mitigate the counselor's duty to convey to the receiving entity that the information in the record is sensitive and confidential.

Prevention and Positive Practice

✓ Discuss access to records during the informed consent process *(see A.2.)*.
✓ When a client who is legally competent requests his or her record, respond cordially and provide access to the record in a timely fashion and in an appropriate setting such as a private room in your office.

- ✓ Know the laws bearing on client access to records in your jurisdiction. Some states and provinces allow clients unfettered access to records regardless of the potential for emotional harm.
- ✓ If a client gives you permission to release his or her record, or if you must release the record for some other reason, make sure the recipients of the record understand that it is confidential.
- ✓ If you have reason to believe that any information in a client's record might actually cause harm (e.g., significant distress or unnecessary shock), consult with a colleague and consider the possibility of withholding all or part of the record should the client request to see it.
- ✓ Before releasing copies of a client's record, be sure to eliminate any direct reference to other clients, such as in the case of group or family counseling.

B.6.g. Storage and Disposal After Termination

> Counselors store records following termination of services to ensure reasonable future access, maintain records in accordance with state and federal statutes governing records, and dispose of client records and other sensitive materials in a manner that protects client confidentiality. When records are of an artistic nature, counselors obtain client (or guardian) consent with regard to the handling of such records or documents. *(See A.1.b.)*

Essential Elements

When a counselor finishes offering services to a client, the obligation to protect that client's record continues for some period. State and federal statutes in each jurisdiction will determine how long client materials must be securely stored before they can legally be destroyed. The records of former clients must be protected with the same rigor as those of current clients. When the time frame specified by law has elapsed, the records of former clients may be disposed of using a technique that ensures their destruction. Should a client's record include any artistic material, it is important to obtain permission from the client or legal guardian before disposing of those materials.

Common Dilemmas and Conflicts

- Lack of awareness of relevant laws specifying the minimum period of record storage following a client's last visit will create risk in this area.
- Counselors who fail to carefully track the time elapsed on stored records may run the risk of failing to destroy records when indicated or may dispose of records prematurely.

Prevention and Positive Practice

- ✓ Abide by state and federal laws for record storage in your jurisdiction.
- ✓ Periodically review stored records and consider disposing of those that have exceeded the minimum period required by law.
- ✓ Only dispose of records in a manner that ensures a client's confidentiality can never be violated.

✓ Remember that this section of the *ACA Code of Ethics* applies to both written material and records stored in any other media.
✓ If a client's record contains any material that might be considered artistic in nature, you are required to seek permission from the client or the client's legal guardian or custodian before destroying it.

B.6.h. Reasonable Precautions

> Counselors take reasonable precautions to protect client confidentiality in the event of the counselor's termination of practice, incapacity, or death. *(See C.2.h.)*

Essential Elements

Responsible counselors plan for the future. This should include planning for one's own incapacity, illness, or death *(see C.2.h.)*. At some point, every counselor will retire or become unable to continue professional work. Wise counselors create a plan for protecting client records in these instances. This may include a professional will that identifies another professional who will inform clients of their counselor's death or incapacitation, address their treatment needs, and maintain or transfer treatment records in these situations.

Common Dilemmas and Conflicts

- Counselors who deny the fact of their own mortality and operate without an explicit contingency plan in the case of their own incapacitation may fail to protect client confidentiality.
- Termination of one's counseling practice does not absolve the counselor of the duty to protect client records.

Prevention and Positive Practice

✓ Take time early in your counseling career to prepare a careful backup plan in the case of your sudden incapacitation or death.
✓ This plan may include a professional will and should designate a professional colleague who agrees to take custody of confidential client records and either store or dispose of them according to ethical standards and legal requirements.
✓ Periodically update your professional will and keep a current copy on hand.
✓ When you terminate your counseling practice because of retirement or illness, inform current clients of your plan well in advance and arrange for appropriate referrals and record transfers for those clients who desire to continue in counseling *(see A.11.)*.

B.7. Research and Training

B.7.a. Institutional Approval

> When institutional approval is required, counselors provide accurate information about their research proposals and obtain approval prior to conducting their research. They conduct research in accordance with the approved research protocol.

B.7.b. Adherence to Guidelines

Counselors are responsible for understanding and adhering to state, federal, agency, or institutional policies or applicable guidelines regarding confidentiality in their research practices.

B.7.c. Confidentiality of Information Obtained in Research

Violations of participant privacy and confidentiality are risks of participation in research involving human participants. Investigators maintain all research records in a secure manner. They explain to participants the risks of violations of privacy and confidentiality and disclose to participants any limits of confidentiality that reasonably can be expected. Regardless of the degree to which confidentiality will be maintained, investigators must disclose to participants any limits of confidentiality that reasonably can be expected. *(See G.2.e.)*

B.7.d. Disclosure of Research Information

Counselors do not disclose confidential information that reasonably could lead to the identification of a research participant unless they have obtained the prior consent of the person. Use of data derived from counseling relationships for purposes of training, research, or publication is confined to content that is disguised to ensure the anonymity of the individuals involved. *(See G.2.a., G.2.d.)*

Essential Elements

When counselors engage in research and other scholarly activities, they protect research participants with the same resolve with which they protect clients. Before undertaking any research effort, counselors carefully review relevant laws and guidelines bearing on research, and they pay special attention to policies on protecting confidentiality. Counselors are also careful to obtain institutional approval for research when this is required; counselors working in agencies, educational settings, and organizations are especially mindful of the requirement to seek institutional approval before collecting any research data. When approval for research is granted, counselors adhere carefully to the approved protocol. Counselors are respectful of research participant privacy and confidentiality. They collect and store research data with thorough attention to protecting the identity and confidentiality of participants and only disclose this information with participants' permission. Finally, counselors provide clear informed consent before engaging a research participant in any way. Informed consent should include information regarding the purpose of the study, potential risks, expected benefits, and the level of confidentiality that participants may expect.

Common Dilemmas and Conflicts

- Counselors who are less experienced with research may easily overlook key ethical and legal requirements.

- It may be tempting to bypass cumbersome institutional approval applications in favor of more "informal" data collection efforts.
- In contrast to their counseling work, counselors may place less emphasis on privacy and confidentiality in their work with research participants.

Prevention and Positive Practice

✓ Take time, before launching a research study, to carefully consider relevant statutes, policies, and guidelines in your jurisdiction and work setting.
✓ Always find out if institutional approval is required before collecting data from any research participant.
✓ Once an approved research study is under way, do not deviate from the approved protocol without explicit permission from the approval-granting entity.
✓ Provide clear informed consent to all research participants *(see G.2.a.)*.
✓ Actively protect participant confidentiality and the confidentiality of all research data *(see G.2.e.)*.
✓ Do not publish or otherwise present research data in a way that might allow for the identification of any research participant unless you first secure written permission from that person.

B.7.e. Agreement for Identification

> Identification of clients, students, or supervisees in a presentation or publication is permissible only when they have reviewed the material and agreed to its presentation or publication. *(See G.4.d.)*

Essential Elements

Counselors who are active as teachers, researchers, and writers may often have reason to use illustrative examples from their counseling and research work. Poignant case examples are often useful in highlighting a principle or demonstrating an approach. But counselors must be cautious not to violate the privacy or confidentiality of a client, student, supervisee, or research participant when making verbal or written presentations *(see G.2.e., G.4.d.)*.

Common Dilemmas and Conflicts

- When a counselor encounters an especially striking, humorous, or memorable case example, it can be tempting to use it for illustrative purposes in a public format.
- Changing a few details about a client or research participant may not be enough to prevent others from identifying the person in a presentation or publication.

Prevention and Positive Practice

✓ Before using any client, student, supervisee, or research participant information or example in a presentation or publication, either disguise the person's identity thoroughly *(see B.7.d.)* or secure the person's written permission.

- ✓ Avoid impromptu stories or examples when giving a presentation.
- ✓ Only use client or research participant examples when you have had adequate time to get permission for such use or change enough of the details that not even the person's family members could recognize the person in your public presentation or writing.

B.8. Consultation

B.8.a. Agreements

When acting as consultants, counselors seek agreements among all parties involved concerning each individual's rights to confidentiality, the obligation of each individual to preserve confidential information, and the limits of confidentiality of information shared by others.

B.8.b. Respect for Privacy

Information obtained in a consulting relationship is discussed for professional purposes only with persons directly involved with the case. Written and oral reports present only data germane to the purposes of the consultation, and every effort is made to protect client identity and to avoid undue invasion of privacy.

B.8.c. Disclosure of Confidential Information

When consulting with colleagues, counselors do not disclose confidential information that reasonably could lead to the identification of a client or other person or organization with whom they have a confidential relationship unless they have obtained the prior consent of the person or organization or the disclosure cannot be avoided. They disclose information only to the extent necessary to achieve the purposes of the consultation. *(See D.2.d.)*

Essential Elements

When counselors serve as consultants, they are vigilant to the potential for confusing or even harmful multiple roles and for intrusions on confidential information shared by various persons in the organization. It is essential that consulting counselors clarify their roles with various members of the organization before beginning any consultation activities. Counselors are also careful to avoid unnecessary intrusions on client privacy when collecting consultation data, and they safeguard the confidentiality of information obtained in the course of the consultation. As in the case of client relationships, counselors obtain consent from an individual in the client organization before disclosing any confidential information regarding that person.

Common Dilemmas and Conflicts

- It may be easy to lose sight of the fact that organizational members also have rights to privacy and confidentiality.
- Failing to clarify roles, expectations, and policies on confidentiality in advance may create misunderstanding and conflict later.

- In the course of giving consultative feedback, counselors may inadvertently share information that allows for the identification of specific individuals.

Prevention and Positive Practice

✓ Be sure you have requisite competence in the role of consultant before accepting work in this area.

✓ Clearly articulate and elicit agreement regarding the roles of all participants in the consultation process.

✓ Clarify your policy on confidential information shared by any member of the organization as well as any limits to confidentiality.

✓ Before making any feedback presentation or preparing a written report for the client organization, carefully check your work to make sure that you are not making any unintended disclosures.

✓ Present only information germane to the consultation; avoid promulgating gossip or including private and irrelevant information.

Section C

Professional Responsibility

Introduction

Counselors aspire to open, honest, and accurate communication in dealing with the public and other professionals. They practice in a nondiscriminatory manner within the boundaries of professional and personal competence and have a responsibility to abide by the *ACA Code of Ethics.* Counselors actively participate in local, state, and national associations that foster the development and improvement of counseling. Counselors advocate to promote change at the individual, group, institutional, and societal levels that improves the quality of life for individuals and groups and removes potential barriers to the provision or access of appropriate services being offered. Counselors have a responsibility to the public to engage in counseling practices that are based on rigorous research methodologies. In addition, counselors engage in self-care activities to maintain and promote their emotional, physical, mental, and spiritual well-being to best meet their professional responsibilities.

C.1. Knowledge of Standards

Counselors have a responsibility to read, understand, and follow the *ACA Code of Ethics* and adhere to applicable laws and regulations.

Essential Elements

Counselors ensure that they are knowledgeable about and follow the dictates of the *ACA Code of Ethics* and relevant laws and regulations. They only offer services within their areas of expertise and competence, and only do so in a nondiscriminatory manner. In all their professional activities, counselors ensure that, whenever feasible, their techniques and interventions have a sound scientific basis. In new areas of counseling practice or in areas for which research support is sparse, counselors follow prevailing standards of practice and well-established theoretical principles. Counselors understand the demands of their professional work and practice ongoing self-care strategies to prevent burnout and professional impairment. Counselors have a professional identity that includes working to promote change on the individual, group, institutional, and societal levels. They use their expertise and training to improve the quality of life of people at all levels of society and work to help ensure unrestricted access to counseling services to all who need them. Counselors participate actively in professional associations to help advance and promote counseling as a profession and as a means of helping others.

Common Dilemmas and Conflicts

- Counselors who rely exclusively on clinical intuition or favorite approaches to counseling may be at risk of overlooking important scientific findings on the efficacy of counseling techniques for specific problems.
- Overlooking one's responsibility to promote change in society and within institutions may contribute to inadequate services for individuals in need.
- Counselors who overlook the need to practice ongoing self-care are at risk of developing impaired professional competence over time.

Prevention and Positive Practice

✓ Remain current on, and integrate into your ongoing counseling practices, the most recent research data on counseling techniques and their effectiveness.

✓ Be familiar with the standards in the *ACA Code of Ethics* and use it as a guide in all your professional work.

✓ Engage in ongoing continuing professional development and education to maintain and enhance your counseling competence, and only practice within your areas of counseling expertise.

✓ Be an active advocate for those in need, working to create organizational and societal change through individual activities and professional association involvement.

✓ Promote competence and wellness by engaging in ongoing self-care practices.

C.2. Professional Competence

C.2.a. Boundaries of Competence

Counselors practice only within the boundaries of their competence, based on their education, training, supervised experience, state and national professional credentials, and appropriate professional experience. Counselors gain knowledge, personal awareness, sensitivity, and skills pertinent to working with a diverse client population. *(See A.9.b., C.4.e., E.2., F.2., F.11.b.)*

C.2.b. New Specialty Areas of Practice

> Counselors practice in specialty areas new to them only after appropriate education, training, and supervised experience. While developing skills in new specialty areas, counselors take steps to ensure the competence of their work and to protect others from possible harm. *(See F.6.f.)*

Essential Elements

As professionals whose work can have a significant impact on the lives of those they serve, counselors carefully develop and maintain competence in the areas in which they practice. Competence means having sufficient knowledge, skill, ability, and experience to effectively deliver a counseling service. Competence requires time to develop and may be acquired through a combination of formal education, counselor training, supervised experience, professional experience, continuing education, and professional licensure and other credentialing. Counselors recognize that competence is a fluid concept; achieving competence at one time does not ensure that one will remain competent over time and as the field evolves. Counselors further recognize that genuine competence requires sensitivity to and awareness of cultural diversity *(see A.2.c., B.1.a.)*; becoming competent in the use of an assessment technique, a counseling approach, or a teaching strategy requires the counselor to understand how each would be appropriately used with clients with different cultural identities (e.g., race, ethnicity, religion, sexual orientation, gender). Counselors also appreciate the fact that competence takes time to develop and requires the integration and application of many discrete competencies. Finally, when counselors embark on a new area of practice, they first take the time required to accumulate the requisite education, training, and supervised experience needed to perform competently in this new role.

Common Dilemmas and Conflicts

- Counselors who overestimate their knowledge and skills may be at risk of practicing outside of their areas of competence, placing clients at risk of harm.
- Failure to seek consultation from colleagues may lead to poor decision making about the limits of one's competence.
- Counselors who focus exclusively on technical skills while ignoring their application with different groups may be lacking in the sensitivity and awareness needed for effectively working with diverse groups of clients.

Prevention and Positive Practice

✓ Consult with experienced colleagues and published professional standards to determine the knowledge and skills needed to provide counseling services in new areas of practice and with new populations.

✓ Ensure a focus on the attitudes, sensitivity, and values needed to competently apply counseling knowledge and skills with diverse populations and in diverse settings.

✓ When expanding areas of counseling practice, always pursue a period of supervised counseling experience with a seasoned expert in this new area of practice.

✓ Remember that if you would not feel comfortable with having colleagues discover you are practicing in a new area, you probably should not be.

C.2.c. Qualified for Employment

Counselors accept employment only for positions for which they are qualified by education, training, supervised experience, state and national professional credentials, and appropriate professional experience. Counselors hire for professional counseling positions only individuals who are qualified and competent for those positions.

C.2.d. Monitor Effectiveness

Counselors continually monitor their effectiveness as professionals and take steps to improve when necessary. Counselors in private practice take reasonable steps to seek peer supervision as needed to evaluate their efficacy as counselors.

C.2.e. Consultation on Ethical Obligations

Counselors take reasonable steps to consult with other counselors or related professionals when they have questions regarding their ethical obligations or professional practice.

Essential Elements

When accepting employment positions and when hiring others for professional counseling positions, counselors ensure that they and those they hire have the range and level of competence needed for effectively carrying out the anticipated counseling duties in these positions. Counselors have an ethical responsibility to monitor their professional functioning and competence on an ongoing basis, limit their counseling services when necessary, and obtain the needed education, training, and supervision to maintain needed competence *(see C.2.a.)*. Counselors in private practice may face an additional challenge of professional isolation, and they seek peer supervision to assist in evaluating their professional competence and effectiveness. When professional questions arise and when faced with ethics dilemmas, counselors consult with colleagues as one component of efforts to resolve these matters in keeping with the best interests of those they serve.

Common Dilemmas and Conflicts

- Experienced counselors who have been in practice for many years, and those who practice independently, may overlook the need to self-monitor their effectiveness and to consult with others regarding ongoing training needs.
- Financial pressures or a strong desire to either obtain or fill an employment position may diminish counselors' judgment about their own or others' actual level of preparation and competence for a particular position.

- Counselors with limited experience addressing ethics dilemmas may fail to understand the complexity of some counseling situations and the need to secure good consultation to protect client welfare.

Prevention and Positive Practice

✓ Accurately assess the competencies needed for employment positions and conduct a thorough and fair assessment of each applicant's competence when making hiring decisions.

✓ Before accepting an offer for a new counseling position, ensure that you are competent to do the job by virtue of your education, training, and supervised experience.

✓ If you do not possess the requisite competence for a new counseling position, accept the job only if you can arrange the oversight, supervision, and ongoing training necessary to ensure your competence.

✓ Enlist the assistance of experienced and trusted colleagues to help in assessing and monitoring your competence and ongoing training needs over time.

✓ When ethics dilemmas or challenges arise in counseling practice, consult with an experienced colleague for input and advice on how best to proceed.

C.2.f. Continuing Education

> Counselors recognize the need for continuing education to acquire and maintain a reasonable level of awareness of current scientific and professional information in their fields of activity. They take steps to maintain competence in the skills they use, are open to new procedures, and keep current with the diverse populations and specific populations with whom they work.

Essential Elements

Counseling is a dynamic and vibrant field that is continually evolving. New research findings are published regularly, the scope and role of counselors expand, information and skills learned years ago become obsolete, and counselors expand their practices into new roles and settings and work with new populations. Counselors therefore need to continually and deliberately maintain existing competence. They must also develop or expand competence as needed to effectively provide counseling services with diverse populations, in a wide range of settings, and through new and evolving roles.

Common Dilemmas and Conflicts

- An overreliance on past training and outdated experience may leave counselors vulnerable to deteriorating competence over time.
- Failure to remain current on changes in the counseling field may result in clients receiving substandard care.
- Those who expand their counseling practices into new areas or who begin work with new populations without first obtaining the needed education and training are at risk for harming clients and for violating this *Code of Ethics*.

Prevention and Positive Practice

- ✓ Consult with experienced colleagues and published standards to determine the additional education and training needed before expanding your counseling practice into new areas or working in new roles.
- ✓ Actively seek out specialized education and training needed to competently counsel clients with diverse cultural backgrounds.
- ✓ Realize that competence is dynamic and must be attended to on an ongoing basis to ensure it does not deteriorate.
- ✓ Make continuing education an ongoing aspect of your professional life.

C.2.g. Impairment

Counselors are alert to the signs of impairment from their own physical, mental, or emotional problems and refrain from offering or providing professional services when such impairment is likely to harm a client or others. They seek assistance for problems that reach the level of professional impairment, and, if necessary, they limit, suspend, or terminate their professional responsibilities until such time as it is determined that they may safely resume their work. Counselors assist colleagues or supervisors in recognizing their own professional impairment and provide consultation and assistance when warranted with colleagues or supervisors showing signs of impairment and intervene as appropriate to prevent imminent harm to clients. *(See A.11.b., F.8.b.)*

C.2.h. Counselor Incapacitation or Termination of Practice

When counselors leave a practice, they follow a prepared plan for transfer of clients and files. Counselors prepare and disseminate to an identified colleague or "records custodian" a plan for the transfer of clients and files in the case of their incapacitation, death, or termination of practice.

Essential Elements

All counselors are susceptible to impaired professional competence because of the challenging nature of their work, the demands of personal lives, their own personality characteristics, and varying ability to cope with and manage stress. Like all people, counselors are vulnerable to many challenges and life stressors. Counselors must be mindful of their vulnerabilities; this necessitates the development of reasonable personal insight. When counselors' competence ebbs or when they become impaired, they seek professional consultation and take actions to safeguard the best interests of those they serve. In response to problems of professional competence, counselors may limit, suspend, or terminate their counseling activities as needed; seek professional assistance; or obtain ongoing supervision. As responsible colleagues, counselors are equally alert to signs of impaired competence in their colleagues and take appropriate actions as needed to support them while helping to protect their clients *(see H.2.b.)*. In anticipation of the fact that counselors may at some point in time need to withdraw from practice or may be unable to carry out their counseling duties, a colleague is identified who will take responsibility for records transfer to ensure continuity of care for clients *(see A.11., B.6.h.)*.

Common Dilemmas and Conflicts

- Counselors who feel invulnerable or have an inflated sense of their coping abilities may overlook or minimize warning signs of distress and thus be at increased risk of impaired professional competence.
- Counselors experiencing financial stress may be unwilling to limit or suspend practice, even when this is clearly indicated.
- Counselors who overlook colleagues' impaired functioning place clients at risk of harm.
- Failure to recognize and accept the potential for incapacitation or withdrawal from practice in the future may result in neglecting to identify a records custodian and subsequent disruption in clients' counseling.

Prevention and Positive Practice

✓ Practice ongoing self-care and utilize self-monitoring of personal, emotional, and physical functioning to prevent burnout and impaired professional competence.

✓ Be cognizant of colleagues' professional functioning and be alert to signs of their distress and impairment. When such signs are present, intervene in a thoughtful and caring manner.

✓ When signs of impairment are present, consult with experienced colleagues and then follow their recommendations regarding needed interventions and assistance.

✓ Always consider the impact of decisions on client care.

✓ Make arrangements with a colleague to be custodian of clinical records, contact clients, and transfer records as needed should you become incapacitated or unable to continue in counseling practice.

C.3. Advertising and Soliciting Clients

C.3.a. Accurate Advertising

When advertising or otherwise representing their services to the public, counselors identify their credentials in an accurate manner that is not false, misleading, deceptive, or fraudulent.

C.3.b. Testimonials

Counselors who use testimonials do not solicit them from current clients nor former clients nor any other persons who may be vulnerable to undue influence.

C.3.c. Statements by Others

Counselors make reasonable efforts to ensure that statements made by others about them or the profession of counseling are accurate.

Essential Elements

To inform the public about the services they provide, many counselors advertise their professional services. It is vital that all advertisements be accurate and truthful so they do not mislead vulnerable individuals. While testimonial endorsements are used by some professionals in their advertising, counselors do not solicit testimonials from current or former clients or any other person who may be vulnerable to their influence. Although this standard does not totally rule out the possibility of using unsolicited testimonials in advertising, counselors who use them take great care to ensure that they in no way take advantage of the individual offering the testimonial or create a conflict of interest situation. When others make public statements about a counselor or about the counseling profession that are not accurate, counselors take reasonable steps to correct the information.

Common Dilemmas and Conflicts

- Counselors who are overly focused on practice development or expansion may be at risk for using testimonial endorsements by clients in their advertising.
- Counselors using testimonial endorsements are at risk of a conflict of interest wherein they put their own best interests ahead of the client's.
- Delegating responsibility for the content of counseling services advertisements to others increases the risk that inaccurate information may be shared with the public.

Prevention and Positive Practice

✓ Always consider clients' and former clients' best interests and only use testimonial endorsements in advertising with great caution.
✓ Remember that using client testimonials will often create a perception of exploitation and impropriety, even if this is not the case.
✓ Counselors should ensure that all public statements, including advertising materials, are fully accurate and truthful.
✓ When delegating responsibility for creating advertising materials, counselors accept final responsibility for the content and ensure each ad's accuracy.

C.3.d. Recruiting Through Employment

> Counselors do not use their places of employment or institutional affiliation to recruit or gain clients, supervisees, or consultees for their private practices.

Essential Elements

When a counselor is employed by an agency or institution, there is an implied contract that all professional activities in that setting will be conducted with that agency's or institution's best interests in mind. To exploit one's role with an organization or agency to recruit clients, supervisees, or consultees for personal gain—often to build one's private practice—violates the spirit and the letter of the *ACA Code of Ethics.*

Common Dilemmas and Conflicts

- Counselors striving to build a private practice while working as employees may be tempted to use the agency's or institution's clients for this purpose.
- Those with significant ambitions or financial pressures may be at risk for violating this standard.

Prevention and Positive Practice

✓ Always act in accordance with your employment contract.
✓ Never encourage organizational clients to seek services in your private practice.
✓ Keep in mind that generating clients from an employment setting for one's private practice may amount to putting your financial needs and interests ahead of those of clients, the institution, and your profession.

C.3.e. Products and Training Advertisements

Counselors who develop products related to their profession or conduct workshops or training events ensure that the advertisements concerning these products or events are accurate and disclose adequate information for consumers to make informed choices. *(See C.6.d.)*

C.3.f. Promoting to Those Served

Counselors do not use counseling, teaching, training, or supervisory relationships to promote their products or training events in a manner that is deceptive or would exert undue influence on individuals who may be vulnerable. However, counselor educators may adopt textbooks they have authored for instructional purposes.

Essential Elements

Many counselors develop and sell products such as books, assessment tools, seminars, continuing education workshops, and the like. It is important that counselors take responsibility to ensure that all advertisements for these products and services are accurate. Counselors share sufficient information so that consumers can make a fully informed decision about purchasing these products or participating in these activities. When sharing this information with clients, supervisees, and students, counselors do not take advantage of their dependence and vulnerability. Counselors make efforts to ensure that clients, supervisees, and students are not coerced or exploited. The adoption of a textbook authored by the counselor for a class she or he teaches is not included in these cautionary statements as long as the textbook is appropriate for the learning needs of the students and consistent with the learning objectives of the course.

Common Dilemmas and Conflicts

- Counselors who are highly entrepreneurial and focused on financial success are more likely to take advantage of clients, students, and supervisees by influencing them to purchase the counselors' products.
- Counselors who delegate advertising duties to others may find that their products and services are misrepresented to the public.

Prevention and Positive Practice

✓ Take responsibility for the content of advertising material and always ensure its accuracy.

- ✓ Never pressure clients, supervisees, or students to purchase your goods or use your services, even when your products and services seem appropriate for them.
- ✓ Always disclose adequate information so that those considering purchases may make a fully informed decision.
- ✓ Never take advantage of the dependence or vulnerability of clients, supervisees, or students.

C.4. Professional Qualifications

C.4.a. Accurate Representation

Counselors claim or imply only professional qualifications actually completed and correct any known misrepresentations of their qualifications by others. Counselors truthfully represent the qualifications of their professional colleagues. Counselors clearly distinguish between paid and volunteer work experience and accurately describe their continuing education and specialized training. *(See C.2.a.)*

C.4.b. Credentials

Counselors claim only licenses or certifications that are current and in good standing.

C.4.c. Educational Degrees

Counselors clearly differentiate between earned and honorary degrees.

C.4.d. Implying Doctoral-Level Competence

Counselors clearly state their highest earned degree in counseling or a closely related field. Counselors do not imply doctoral-level competence when only possessing a master's degree in counseling or a related field or by referring to themselves as "Dr." in a counseling context when their doctorate is not in counseling or a related field.

C.4.e. Program Accreditation Status

Counselors clearly state the accreditation status of their degree programs at the time the degree was earned.

C.4.f. Professional Membership

Counselors clearly differentiate between current, active memberships and former memberships in associations. Members of the American Counseling Association must clearly differentiate between professional membership, which implies the possession of at least a master's degree in counseling, and regular membership, which is open to individuals whose interests and activities are consistent with those of ACA but are not qualified for professional membership.

Essential Elements

The stature of the counseling profession hinges on the honesty and integrity with which counselors interface with consumers. In representing themselves to the public, counselors share their credentials and degrees accurately, do not misrepresent credentials, and do not misrepresent colleagues' credentials. Only those with a doctoral degree in counseling or a closely related field represent themselves to the public as "Dr." Counselors accurately portray the accreditation status of their training program at the time of their graduation. Volunteer work is not presented as paid work experience, and all competencies and training experiences are described accurately. Professional association memberships, licensure status, and degree completion are all presented accurately to the public and one's level of membership is not misrepresented. Counselors only report credentials and memberships that are current.

Common Dilemmas and Conflicts

- Counselors who are focused on achieving status or obtaining as many referrals as possible may be at risk of misrepresenting credentials, training, and professional association membership.
- Counselors with powerful needs for aggrandizement are especially vulnerable in this area.
- Those whose training program obtained accreditation after they graduated may be tempted to claim graduation from an accredited program.

Prevention and Positive Practice

✓ Always present all credentials and certifications accurately based on their current status.

✓ Ensure that the public is not misled by incomplete or inaccurate information regarding your education, training, and experience.

✓ If you discover inadequate or erroneous information about yourself in a public forum, correct this at once so that the public is accurately informed.

✓ Never claim certifications, degrees, specialized training and competencies, or memberships that are not current and accurate.

C.5. Nondiscrimination

> Counselors do not condone or engage in discrimination based on age, culture, disability, ethnicity, race, religion/spirituality, gender, gender identity, sexual orientation, marital status/partnership, language preference, socioeconomic status, or any basis proscribed by law. Counselors do not discriminate against clients, students, employees, supervisees, or research participants in a manner that has a negative impact on these persons.

Essential Elements

Counselors are always attentive to, and respectful of, individual differences. Counselors do not discriminate based on individual differences in their professional activities and ensure the well-being and appropriate treatment of all those they interact with in their professional roles *(see A.1.a, A.4.a.)*. Counselors are knowledgeable of the many forms of diversity and find ways to communicate genuine respect for the client.

Common Dilemmas and Conflicts

- Counselors who lack sensitivity to the experiences of individuals of diverse backgrounds may be at risk of unfairly discriminating against them.
- Counselors who hold prejudicial and stereotyped views of persons representing specific groups may be more inclined to discriminate against them.

Prevention and Positive Practice

✓ Develop and maintain ongoing competence in counseling, supervising, training, and researching individuals of diverse backgrounds.

✓ Remain mindful of each client's rights, worldview, and experiences based on membership in specific cultural groups.

✓ Carefully evaluate your own selection criteria and counseling outcomes to ensure that members of specific demographic groups are not disadvantaged when seeking or engaging you for services.

C.6. Public Responsibility

C.6.a. Sexual Harassment

Counselors do not engage in or condone sexual harassment. Sexual harassment is defined as sexual solicitation, physical advances, or verbal or nonverbal conduct that is sexual in nature, that occurs in connection with professional activities or roles, and that either

1. is unwelcome, is offensive, or creates a hostile workplace or learning environment, and counselors know or are told this; or
2. is sufficiently severe or intense to be perceived as harassment to a reasonable person in the context in which the behavior occurred.

Sexual harassment can consist of a single intense or severe act or multiple persistent or pervasive acts.

Essential Elements

Counselors do not engage in or condone sexual harassment. Counselors are knowledgeable of the definition of sexual harassment and understand the corrosive effect sexual harassment can have on individual clients and work environments. Counselors actively work to ensure that no individual or group with whom they work is exposed to sexual harassment.

Common Dilemmas and Conflicts

- Counselors not sensitive to, and knowledgeable of, sexual harassment may inadvertently carry out or condone harassing acts.
- Immature counselors and counselors with lower levels of personal insight may be more prone to sexual harassment.

- When a counselor blurs roles and attempts to romanticize a professional relationship, the risk of sexual harassment increases.

Prevention and Positive Practice

✓ Know the definition of sexual harassment and actively work to prevent it in the workplace.
✓ Avoid the use of sexual humor or teasing in any professional relationship or setting.
✓ Recognize that personal distress and loneliness may increase the risk for sexual harassment.
✓ When in a supervisory or leadership role, ensure that all subordinates are trained about these issues and ensure their compliance.

C.6.b. Reports to Third Parties

Counselors are accurate, honest, and objective in reporting their professional activities and judgments to appropriate third parties, including courts, health insurance companies, those who are the recipients of evaluation reports, and others. *(See B.3., E.4.)*

C.6.c. Media Presentations

When counselors provide advice or comment by means of public lectures, demonstrations, radio or television programs, prerecorded tapes, technology-based applications, printed articles, mailed material, or other media, they take reasonable precautions to ensure that

1. the statements are based on appropriate professional counseling literature and practice,
2. the statements are otherwise consistent with the *ACA Code of Ethics,* and
3. the recipients of the information are not encouraged to infer that a professional counseling relationship has been established.

Essential Elements

There are numerous occasions when counselors are called upon to make reports to third parties, such as when giving depositions, testifying in court, sharing information with managed care or health insurance companies (e.g., requesting authorizations, justifying a diagnosis or treatment plan), or sharing reports of counseling or assessments with others such as schools or employers. In each of these situations counselors must be vigilant to ensure that all information, whether shared verbally or in written reports, is fully truthful, accurate, and not misleading. Additionally, when sharing information in any public forum, regardless of the medium used, counselors ensure that all statements are consistent with current counseling literature, prevailing standards of practice, and the *ACA Code of Ethics.* Further, counselors make reasonable efforts to ensure that those receiving information through public media do not infer a professional relationship when one does not exist. It is important that those receiving this information in a public forum do not interpret it as personal advice specifically relevant to their individual circumstances.

Common Dilemmas and Conflicts

- Counselors feeling pressure to justify their work or recommendations in a public forum may be tempted to make statements that go beyond the limits of their data, experience, or competence.
- Counselors working in the media may feel pressure to be entertaining and may offer advice or recommendations that are inconsistent with prevailing professional standards.
- Counselors justifying their diagnoses and treatment plans to insurance personnel may be at risk of overpathologizing clients in an effort to obtain needed treatment authorizations.

Prevention and Positive Practice

✓ Always present professional opinions and conclusions accurately and objectively when making a report to any third party.

✓ Never make statements or render opinions that go beyond available data; ask yourself whether a jury of your peers would agree.

✓ Be sure that your public statements and presentations are consistent with currently available professional counseling literature and standards.

✓ Media presentations should not suggest a professional relationship with members of the public who solicit advice; make an effort to ensure that your advice is not misconstrued as a replacement for sound professional counseling.

C.6.d. Exploitation of Others

Counselors do not exploit others in their professional relationships. *(See C.3.e.)*

C.6.e. Scientific Bases for Treatment Modalities

Counselors use techniques/procedures/modalities that are grounded in theory and/or have an empirical or scientific foundation. Counselors who do not must define the techniques/procedures as "unproven" or "developing" and explain the potential risks and ethical considerations of using such techniques/procedures and take steps to protect clients from possible harm. *(See A.4.a., E.5.c., E.5.d.)*

Essential Elements

Counselors accept and understand the power differentials inherent in their professional relationships and do not ever exploit others with whom they interact professionally. Counselors recognize that exploitation may take many forms from overt and egregious (e.g., coercing sexual favors, bilking a client financially) to subtle and difficult to identify (e.g., using a client to get one's emotional needs met). All techniques, procedures, and modalities of counseling must be based on accepted scientific literature and prevailing professional practice standards. All unproven techniques, procedures, and modalities and those that are in some phase of development must be presented as unproven or experimental. All reasonably anticipated potential risks of participation must be disclosed up front *(see A.2.)*, and counselors must take active steps to protect clients from harm.

Common Dilemmas and Conflicts

- Counselors who are emotionally needy or eager for financial success may be at greater risk for exploitation.
- Those developing new counseling approaches and assessment techniques may be so eager to promote their use that they either overlook or minimize the potential risks involved.
- Those developing new counseling approaches and assessment techniques may minimize or ignore potential risks in an effort to hasten research or dissemination of their work.

Prevention and Positive Practice

✓ Remain cognizant of the potential for exploitation of clients, attend to their vulnerabilities, and consider their best interests in all professional decisions.
✓ Present all unproven or developing techniques and strategies accurately and ensure that clients are fully informed of all potential risks prior to their participation.
✓ When using unproven or developing techniques and strategies, monitor their impact on clients closely and take active steps to prevent harm to clients.

C.7. Responsibility to Other Professionals

C.7.a. Personal Public Statements

> When making personal statements in a public context, counselors clarify that they are speaking from their personal perspectives and that they are not speaking on behalf of all counselors or the profession.

Essential Elements

When making public statements of a personal nature, counselors clarify that their statements are their own and not representative of any professional organization, other counselors, or the profession of counseling at large. For instance, a counselor should never insinuate that he or she speaks for the American Counseling Association without explicit permission from that organization.

Common Dilemmas and Conflicts

- Counselors working with the media may fail to clearly distinguish personal opinion from scientific evidence or prevailing professional standards.
- Counselors who feel defensive or who seek public notoriety may be tempted to make personal remarks as though they are representative of the field of counseling or a counseling organization.

Prevention and Positive Practice

✓ Always preface personal statements to the public as your own opinions and beliefs, ensuring that there is no implication of speaking for other counselors or the profession.
✓ Consider the impact of your public comments on your peers and your profession.
✓ When preparing to make a public statement, have a trusted colleague review it first.

Section D

Relationships With Other Professionals

Introduction

Professional counselors recognize that the quality of their interactions with colleagues can influence the quality of services provided to clients. They work to become knowledgeable about colleagues within and outside the field of counseling. Counselors develop positive working relationships and systems of communication with colleagues to enhance services to clients.

Essential Elements

Counselors may interact, consult, and work with a wide range of professionals in their efforts to provide clients with the highest possible level of care. Examples may include interactions with a psychologist who conducts a neuropsychological evaluation of a client, a psychiatrist who provides medication to a client, a social worker who assists with aftercare arrangements, and a primary care physician who conducts a physical evaluation of a client. Counselors intentionally develop such relationships and communicate effectively with these professionals to ensure the best possible care for their clients.

Common Dilemmas and Conflicts

- Counselors who feel jealous of or competitive with other professionals may minimize the importance of other professionals' roles.
- Counselors who overestimate their knowledge and abilities may overlook the importance of other professionals' roles in ensuring the best possible care for clients.

- Counselors who are unfamiliar with the unique competencies associated with each mental health profession may overlook the potential contributions of other professionals.

Prevention and Positive Practice

✓ Value and respect the roles and potential contributions of other professionals to your clients' care and welfare.
✓ Take steps to develop and maintain good working relationships with other professionals involved in clients' care.
✓ Actively seek out the input and involvement of allied professionals as indicated by each client's specific needs.
✓ Educate yourself about the role each colleague can play in a client's health and well-being.

D.1. Relationships With Colleagues, Employers, and Employees

D.1.a. Different Approaches

Counselors are respectful of approaches to counseling services that differ from their own. Counselors are respectful of traditions and practices of other professional groups with which they work.

D.1.b. Forming Relationships

Counselors work to develop and strengthen interdisciplinary relations with colleagues from other disciplines to best serve clients.

Essential Elements

Counselors deliberately forge collegial working relationships with a wide range of professionals to ensure that clients receive the best possible care. Counselors recognize and respect colleagues' differing viewpoints, approaches, and strategies, both within the counseling profession and in allied professions; counselors put away theoretical and disciplinary differences in the service of professional collaboration. Counselors are mindful of the ways in which positive and collegial relationships among professionals help to maximize the quality of services for clients, and they do not hesitate to refer clients to allied professionals when this would be in clients' best interests.

Common Dilemmas and Conflicts

- Looking down on or disregarding the potential contributions of colleagues in other professions may result in inadequate client care.
- Failing to work collaboratively or engaging in turf battles may cause important theoretical perspectives and treatment approaches to be overlooked.
- Counselors who are rigid adherents to a single counseling theory or technique may be at risk in this area.

Prevention and Positive Practice

- ✓ Always treat colleagues from other professions with respect and value their potential contributions to clients' care.
- ✓ Place your client's best interests before professional ego or turf.
- ✓ Remain open to different counseling approaches and perspectives, especially those with which you may be unfamiliar.
- ✓ Actively work to develop collaborative relationships with other professionals so that clients' best interests are served.

D.1.c. Interdisciplinary Teamwork

Counselors who are members of interdisciplinary teams delivering multifaceted services to clients keep the focus on how to best serve the clients. They participate in and contribute to decisions that affect the well-being of clients by drawing on the perspectives, values, and experiences of the counseling profession and those of colleagues from other disciplines. *(See A.1.a.)*

D.1.d. Confidentiality

When counselors are required by law, institutional policy, or extraordinary circumstances to serve in more than one role in judicial or administrative proceedings, they clarify role expectations and the parameters of confidentiality with their colleagues. *(See B.1.c., B.1.d., B.2.c., B.2.d., B.3.b.)*

D.1.e. Establishing Professional and Ethical Obligations

Counselors who are members of interdisciplinary teams clarify professional and ethical obligations of the team as a whole and of its individual members. When a team decision raises ethical concerns, counselors first attempt to resolve the concern within the team. If they cannot reach resolution among team members, counselors pursue other avenues to address their concerns consistent with client well-being.

Essential Elements

Ethics challenges may arise in a range of settings and circumstances. Counselors on interdisciplinary treatment teams work collaboratively with colleagues to bring the best from each profession involved to the task of serving clients' best interests. In such interdisciplinary settings, counselors approach colleagues from diverse disciplines with a spirit of cooperation. When counselors serve in judicial or administrative proceedings, they may be required to serve in more than one role. When this occurs it is essential that they first clarify any limits to confidentiality with their professional colleagues. For example, when a counselor serves as an individual's supervisor and also sits on an administrative review board for that supervisee, the supervisee has the right to know in advance whether information from one role or context may be shared in the other. When counselors working on interdisciplinary treatment teams suspect an ethical violation has occurred within the team, or that a team decision may violate a client's best interests, they first try to resolve the problem directly with the team members involved. If this proves ineffective or is not possible, other steps may be taken, such as filing a formal ethics complaint.

Common Dilemmas and Conflicts

- Marginalizing or ignoring the potential contributions of other mental health professionals may undermine the value of a multidisciplinary team.
- Counselors who assume that professional colleagues share an understanding of the potential limits to confidentiality in a treatment team context may contribute to a violation of client confidentiality.
- Rushing to file a formal ethics complaint instead of trying to resolve a team-related matter directly with the individuals involved will often lead to unnecessary negative outcomes.

Prevention and Positive Practice

✓ Actively solicit and integrate the perspectives, values, and experiences of colleagues from both counseling and allied mental health professions.
✓ Explain to colleagues early on how your professional roles and obligations will affect the limits to client confidentiality.
✓ When working on a treatment team, clarify the ethical obligations of individual team members and of the team overall at the outset.
✓ When ethics concerns arise in the course of multidisciplinary team work, first clarify relevant issues and express concerns directly to your colleagues.
✓ If efforts at informal resolution of ethical concerns are ineffective, then consider alternative approaches to protecting client interests (e.g., filing a formal complaint).

D.1.f. Personnel Selection and Assignment

Counselors select competent staff and assign responsibilities compatible with their skills and experiences.

D.1.g. Employer Policies

The acceptance of employment in an agency or institution implies that counselors are in agreement with its general policies and principles. Counselors strive to reach agreement with employers as to acceptable standards of conduct that allow for changes in institutional policy conducive to the growth and development of clients.

D.1.h. Negative Conditions

Counselors alert their employers of inappropriate policies and practices. They attempt to effect changes in such policies or procedures through constructive action within the organization. When such policies are potentially disruptive or damaging to clients or may limit the effectiveness of services provided and change cannot be effected, counselors take appropriate further action. Such action may include referral to appropriate certification, accreditation, or state licensure organizations, or voluntary termination of employment.

D.1.i. Protection From Punitive Action

Counselors take care not to harass or dismiss an employee who has acted in a responsible and ethical manner to expose inappropriate employer policies or practices.

Essential Elements

Counselors who work in agencies or institutions have a number of responsibilities. Counselors should carefully review and understand the implications of all employment contracts, policies, and administrative expectations before accepting any employment; acceptance of employment implies agreement with these policies and expectations. Counselors work to ensure that all organizational policies and procedures are consistent with the dictates of this *ACA Code of Ethics* and that they are consistent with clients' best interests *(see A.1.a)*. If policies, expectations, or work conditions are not appropriate, acceptable, or consistent with this *Code of Ethics*, counselors take appropriate actions to effect a remedy, first within the organization, but if necessary with other agencies and oversight organizations. When supervising others, counselors only delegate those tasks that subordinates are competent to perform based on their education, training, and experience. When an employee brings unethical or inappropriate practices to a counselor's attention, the employee is never harassed or fired as a result of this action.

Common Dilemmas and Conflicts

- Those who are desperate to obtain employment may fail to give employment policies and requirements adequate scrutiny.
- Concern about jeopardizing one's employment status may underlie a counselor's willingness to overlook or condone inappropriate work practices.
- Supervising counselors who feel significant financial or organizational pressure to provide a high volume of services may be at risk of delegating tasks to subordinates who do not possess the needed competence to effectively carry out those tasks.
- A counselor who feels threatened and angered by a subordinate's report of unethical policies or practices is at increased risk of unethical retribution against the subordinate.

Prevention and Positive Practice

✓ Review all employment contracts, administrative policies, and employment expectations prior to accepting a new position.

✓ When you become aware of unjust, unethical, or potentially harmful practices, procedures, or expectations in an employment situation, bring these to the attention of senior personnel and work to remedy them.

✓ When efforts to promote needed change within an agency are not effective, contact external agencies with oversight authority to effect needed change.

✓ If an employee makes a report of inappropriate policies or practices to you, take these allegations seriously, work collaboratively with this employee to promote and effect needed change, and never respond punitively.

✓ Always carefully assess subordinates' competencies before delegating tasks and responsibilities so that work expectations are consistent with their competence and skills.

D.2. Consultation

D.2.a. Consultant Competency

Counselors take reasonable steps to ensure that they have the appropriate resources and competencies when providing consultation services. Counselors provide appropriate referral resources when requested or needed. *(See C.2.a.)*

D.2.b. Understanding Consultees

When providing consultation, counselors attempt to develop with their consultees a clear understanding of problem definition, goals for change, and predicted consequences of interventions selected.

D.2.c. Consultant Goals

The consulting relationship is one in which consultee adaptability and growth toward self-direction are consistently encouraged and cultivated.

Essential Elements

Counselors work in a wide range of settings and professional roles. When working as consultants to others, counselors first ensure that they possess the needed competence to serve in this role. When clients' needs exceed the counselors' competence, counselors make referrals as needed. Counselors carefully assess each consultee's needs prior to making recommendations. Counselors thoughtfully develop and present a consultation plan to consultees for their approval prior to its implementation. Consulting plans always include a description of the problem to be addressed, goals for change, and anticipated outcomes. The overarching goal of each counselor consultant is the consultee's growth toward effective and self-sufficient functioning.

Common Dilemmas and Conflicts

- Counselors focused on expanding sources of income may be more likely to provide consultation services before developing the needed competence.
- Counselors who are driven by financial considerations or who are grandiose in their self-assessment of competence may continue providing consultation services when a referral to a more appropriate consultant is needed.
- Counselors who are hierarchical—versus collaborative—in their approach to consultation may fail to include consultees in the development and approval of an appropriate consultation plan.

Prevention and Positive Practice

✓ Prior to offering consultation services, obtain the education, training, and supervised experience needed to ensure your competence.

✓ Carefully assess each consultee's needs and develop a consultation plan that is reviewed with the consultee prior to offering any interventions.

- ✓ When consultee needs exceed your competence or the range of services that you are prepared to offer, make appropriate referrals to ensure that the consultee's best interests are served.
- ✓ Periodically review your consultation cases to ensure that each consultee's growth and self-direction are facilitated by your work; increasing consultee dependence should be cause for concern.

D.2.d. Informed Consent in Consultation

When providing consultation, counselors have an obligation to review, in writing and verbally, the rights and responsibilities of both counselors and consultees. Counselors use clear and understandable language to inform all parties involved about the purpose of the services to be provided, relevant costs, potential risks and benefits, and the limits of confidentiality. Working in conjunction with the consultee, counselors attempt to develop a clear definition of the problem, goals for change, and predicted consequences of interventions that are culturally responsive and appropriate to the needs of consultees. *(See A.2.a., A.2.b.)*

Essential Elements

Just as in all of their other professional roles and with all of their clients, counselors engage in a thoughtful process of information sharing with consultees prior to offering services to ensure fully informed consent *(see A.2.a.)*. Informed consent to consultation should be obtained both verbally and in writing, with careful attention given to sharing all information necessary for consultees to make a well-informed decision about participation in the consultation relationship *(see A.2.b.)*. In developing a consultation plan with a consultee, counselors pay careful attention to individual differences to ensure that a culturally sensitive and appropriate consultation plan is developed. Counselors are mindful of the varied ways in which culture may influence one's understanding of consultative relationships.

Common Dilemmas and Conflicts

- Counselors who feel pressure to implement a consultation plan quickly—whether the pressure is internal or coming from the consultee—may overlook or gloss over the informed consent process.
- Counselors who lack a collaborative approach may neglect consultees' input into developing a comprehensive consultation plan.
- Counselors who forget about cultural differences may fail to provide effective and understandable informed consent for consultation.

Prevention and Positive Practice

- ✓ Always engage in a comprehensive informed consent process prior to providing consultation.
- ✓ Work to ensure that consultees have realistic expectations of the consultation process and that these expectations are addressed verbally and in writing in the informed consent.
- ✓ Actively include stakeholders in developing a consultation plan, incorporating their goals, perspectives, and expectations.
- ✓ Ensure attention to individual differences and relevant cultural and other diversity factors in developing and implementing the consultation plan.

Section E

Evaluation, Assessment, and Interpretation

Introduction

Counselors use assessment instruments as one component of the counseling process, taking into account the client's personal and cultural context. Counselors promote the well-being of individual clients or groups of clients by developing and using appropriate educational, psychological, and career assessment instruments.

Essential Elements

Counselors regularly utilize assessment instruments to assist them in their work with clients. They also recognize both the value and limitations of assessment instruments and techniques; counselors are careful to develop and use assessment instruments only when they are likely to promote the well-being of their clients. In all cases, assessment tools and processes must take into account the unique personal and cultural context of individual clients.

E.1. General

E.1.a. Assessment

The primary purpose of educational, psychological, and career assessment is to provide measurements that are valid and reliable in either comparative or absolute terms. These include, but are not limited to, measurements of ability, personality, interest, intelligence, achievement, and performance. Counselors recognize the need to interpret the statements in this section as applying to both quantitative and qualitative assessments.

E.1.b. Client Welfare

Counselors do not misuse assessment results and interpretations, and they take reasonable steps to prevent others from misusing the information these techniques provide. They respect the client's right to know the results, the interpretations made, and the bases for counselors' conclusions and recommendations.

Essential Elements

Counselors only use assessment tools that are appropriately reliable and valid for the purposes and the individuals in question. The development and use of assessment instruments may add great value to the work of counselors and provide great assistance to clients. Counselors obtain the necessary training to competently administer, score, and interpret assessment instruments; only use them for the purposes and populations for which they are designed; and work to ensure that assessment results are not misused. Counselors recognize that the guidelines in this section apply equally to all forms of assessment, including qualitative techniques. Further, counselors share assessment results, interpretations, and recommendations with clients in a manner that will be of greatest use and value to them.

Common Dilemmas and Conflicts

- Counselors who are ill informed about psychometric measures may rush to utilize assessment techniques that lack appropriate reliability and validity for the individuals and purposes intended.
- Counselors who are unfamiliar with bias inherent in some tests may incorrectly attribute score disparities between the general population and specific minority groups as indicative of actual differences on the variable in question.
- Counselors who neglect making assessment a collaborative process may fail to respect a client's right to fully understand the basis for their counselor's conclusions and recommendations.
- Counselors who accept assessment results uncritically may draw unfounded conclusions and make recommendations that may be harmful to clients.

Prevention and Positive Practice

✓ Always obtain needed training in psychometrics and assessment before using any assessment technique.

✓ Be a thoughtful consumer of assessment techniques, critically examining their intended purpose, reliability, validity, strengths, sources of bias, and limitations.

✓ Always share assessment findings and interpretations with clients in a manner that makes them useful to clients unless nondisclosure was an explicit component of the informed consent agreement.

✓ Only utilize assessment instruments when it is reasonably clear that their results will be of value to the counseling process and beneficial to an individual client.

✓ Be mindful of the limitations of any assessment instrument when interpreting results and drawing conclusions, and take steps to prevent others from misusing or misinterpreting the results as well.

E.2. Competence to Use and Interpret Assessment Instruments

E.2.a. Limits of Competence

Counselors utilize only those testing and assessment services for which they have been trained and are competent. Counselors using technology-assisted test interpretations are trained in the construct being measured and the specific instrument being used prior to using its technology-based application. Counselors take reasonable measures to ensure the proper use of psychological and career assessment techniques by persons under their supervision. *(See A.12.)*

E.2.b. Appropriate Use

Counselors are responsible for the appropriate application, scoring, interpretation, and use of assessment instruments relevant to the needs of the client, whether they score and interpret such assessments themselves or use technology or other services.

E.2.c. Decisions Based on Results

Counselors responsible for decisions involving individuals or policies that are based on assessment results have a thorough understanding of educational, psychological, and career measurement, including validation criteria, assessment research, and guidelines for assessment development and use.

Essential Elements

Assessment techniques may be very helpful in assessing clients' capacities, characteristics, interests, and counseling needs, but counselors must only use them after obtaining the needed training and supervised experience to ensure their competent use. Counselors also ensure that those they supervise or to whom they delegate assessment tasks use assessment techniques appropriately, and they provide sufficient oversight to ensure that assessment instruments are not misused. Although computer-assisted scoring and interpretation services may be time-saving tools, they should be used with care. The counselor maintains ultimate responsibility for assessment results, interpretations, and recommendations even when technology-assisted interpretations are utilized. Counselors ensure that they fully understand the valid uses and limits of each assessment instrument and only make recommendations based on the appropriate interpretation of assessment data.

Common Dilemmas and Conflicts

- Failure to provide subordinates with sufficient training and oversight may result in misuse of assessment instruments and harm to clients.

- A lack of understanding of the psychometric properties of assessment techniques may result in their misuse or in drawing conclusions from results that are not supported by the data.
- Using technology-assisted interpretations as a substitute for professional expertise and judgment may result in misinterpretations and harm to clients.

Prevention and Positive Practice

✓ Select assessment instruments carefully based on their psychometric properties and intended purpose.
✓ Obtain the training needed to be competent prior to utilizing any assessment instrument.
✓ Never go beyond the available data in drawing conclusions or in making interpretations or recommendations.
✓ Remember that assessment data must always be interpreted in light of an individual's unique personal and cultural experience.
✓ Closely supervise subordinates and supervisees to ensure they use assessment instruments competently and appropriately.
✓ Use technology-assisted interpretation services as an adjunct to your clinical judgment, not as a replacement for it.

E.3. Informed Consent in Assessment

E.3.a. Explanation to Clients

Prior to assessment, counselors explain the nature and purposes of assessment and the specific use of results by potential recipients. The explanation will be given in the language of the client (or other legally authorized person on behalf of the client), unless an explicit exception has been agreed upon in advance. Counselors consider the client's personal or cultural context, the level of the client's understanding of the results, and the impact of the results on the client. *(See A.2., A.12.g., F.1.c.)*

E.3.b. Recipients of Results

Counselors consider the examinee's welfare, explicit understandings, and prior agreements in determining who receives the assessment results. Counselors include accurate and appropriate interpretations with any release of individual or group assessment results. *(See B.2.c., B.5.)*

Essential Elements

As with all services they provide, counselors first obtain voluntary informed consent prior to performing assessments of clients. Counselors provide information about the planned assessment in a manner that ensures the client understands the assessment process; counselors obtain informed consent in a collaborative manner that is sensitive to the client's personal and cultural context. This may include attention to the client's intellectual level, culture, language, and other relevant factors. Counselors provide relevant information about the assessment, including who will receive or have access to the results of the assessment, and only release assessment data with appropriate consent. Before releasing assessment data, counselors always refer to explicit understandings and agreements with clients and their best interests. When counselors do release client assessment results, they include accurate and appropriate interpretations of the results.

Common Dilemmas and Conflicts

- Overlooking the informed consent process in assessments or providing only cursory informed consent may violate clients' rights and risk adverse outcomes.
- Failure to clarify from the outset who will have access to assessment results may lead to conflicts, distress, and dissatisfaction.
- Counselors who fail to consider a client's cognitive capacity, culture, language, and other personal variables may fail to obtain genuinely informed consent.

Prevention and Positive Practice

✓ Prior to conducting any assessment, first obtain the client's fully informed consent and ensure that he or she truly understands the information you convey.

✓ Pay particular attention to cultural, intellectual, language, and other factors that might affect the consent process.

✓ Clarify limits to confidentiality and access to test data at the outset.

✓ When sharing assessment results with others, include an appropriate interpretation with the results to help ensure they are not misused or misinterpreted.

E.4. Release of Data to Qualified Professionals

> Counselors release assessment data in which the client is identified only with the consent of the client or the client's legal representative. Such data are released only to persons recognized by counselors as qualified to interpret the data. *(See B.1., B.3.)*

Essential Elements

Counselors do not release client assessment data unless they have obtained formal consent from either the client or the client's legal representative. Even when consent is obtained, counselors collaborate with clients or their legal representatives to determine whether release of test data or results is in the client's best interests. When release of assessment results is deemed ethically and clinically appropriate or is a legal requirement, counselors only release such data to persons whom the counselor deems qualified—by virtue of training and experience—to interpret the data.

Common Dilemmas and Conflicts

- Releasing assessment data to unqualified professionals or others may result in the misinterpretation and misuse of these data.

- Counselors who fail to consider the qualifications of persons to whom they release assessment data may be at risk in this area.

Prevention and Positive Practice

✓ Before releasing test data, ensure the training of the intended recipient so that only those with the ability to competently interpret the data receive them.
✓ Remain current regarding the minimum standards for assessment competence.
✓ If unsure about another professional's competence to interpret assessment data, seek consultation from a colleague in the assessment area.

E.5. Diagnosis of Mental Disorders

E.5.a. Proper Diagnosis

Counselors take special care to provide proper diagnosis of mental disorders. Assessment techniques (including personal interview) used to determine client care (e.g., locus of treatment, type of treatment, or recommended follow-up) are carefully selected and appropriately used.

E.5.b. Cultural Sensitivity

Counselors recognize that culture affects the manner in which clients' problems are defined. Clients' socioeconomic and cultural experiences are considered when diagnosing mental disorders. *(See A.2.c.)*

E.5.c. Historical and Social Prejudices in the Diagnosis of Pathology

Counselors recognize historical and social prejudices in the misdiagnosis and pathologizing of certain individuals and groups and the role of mental health professionals in perpetuating these prejudices through diagnosis and treatment.

E.5.d. Refraining From Diagnosis

Counselors may refrain from making and/or reporting a diagnosis if they believe it would cause harm to the client or others.

Essential Elements

Counselors will frequently be called upon to provide a formal diagnosis of a client. Counselors render a diagnosis only after careful assessment of the client, taking into consideration all relevant factors, including history, presenting problems, symptoms, interview results, and assessment results. Counselors carefully consider cultural and other relevant diversity factors to better understand how culture influences symptoms and clients' understanding of symptoms and to minimize the risk of misdiagnosing clients. Counselors are especially sensitive and thoughtful when diagnosing individuals from backgrounds where historical and social prejudices have resulted in patterns of misdiagnosis in the past, and they work to avoid perpetuating such injustice. For instance, women, African Americans, and sexual minority clients have historically been incorrectly pathologized by mental health practitioners; counselors are careful to avoid perpetuating such inaccuracies. When it appears that providing a client with a diagnosis might result in harm to that client, counselors may refrain from making or reporting a diagnosis for that individual *(see A.1.a., A.4.a.).*

Common Dilemmas and Conflicts

- Labeling a client with a diagnosis after only a cursory assessment may result in misdiagnosis and harm.
- Counselors who fail to render proper diagnoses informed by appropriate assessment strategies are at risk of creating a misguided counseling plan.
- Providing or reporting a diagnosis for every client regardless of the potential for harm to clients may be unethical.
- Counselors who assume that the diagnostic criteria of the *Diagnostic and Statistical Manual of Mental Disorders* (4th ed., Text Revision [*DSM–IV–TR*]; American Psychiatric Association, 2000) can be applied to all clients may overlook cultural factors rendering the *DSM* criteria less accurate with some clients and contexts.
- Overlooking historical patterns of misdiagnosis or allowing prejudices and bias to influence the diagnosis process can perpetuate harmful patterns of misdiagnosis and harm.

Prevention and Positive Practice

✓ Carefully consider all relevant factors and conduct a thorough assessment before providing a diagnosis for any client.
✓ Be sure to abide by state and provincial laws bearing on requirements for and limitations on diagnosis by counselors.
✓ Ensure that all diagnoses are accurate, based on current client information, and updated as indicated by the clinical evidence.
✓ Consider the potential impact on the client before making or reporting a diagnosis.
✓ Always consider cultural and other relevant diversity factors when making a diagnosis.
✓ When working with a client from a cultural group that has traditionally been disadvantaged by the mental health system, give extra attention to avoiding pathologizing and misdiagnosis.
✓ If you lack competence in the assessment and diagnosis of members of a specific cultural group, seek appropriate consultation and supervision before proceeding.

E.6. Instrument Selection

E.6.a. Appropriateness of Instruments

Counselors carefully consider the validity, reliability, psychometric limitations, and appropriateness of instruments when selecting assessments.

E.6.b. Referral Information

If a client is referred to a third party for assessment, the counselor provides specific referral questions and sufficient objective data about the client to ensure that appropriate assessment instruments are utilized. *(See A.9.b., B.3.)*

E.6.c. Culturally Diverse Populations

Counselors are cautious when selecting assessments for culturally diverse populations to avoid the use of instruments that lack appropriate psychometric properties for the client population. *(See A.2.c., E.5.b.)*

Essential Elements

When selecting assessment instruments for use in counseling practice, counselors carefully consider the psychometric properties of each instrument to determine the appropriateness of its use. Factors such as reliability and validity, the population on which the instrument was normed, and any psychometric limitations each should be considered. When selecting assessment instruments for use with diverse populations, counselors first ensure that the assessment instruments possess appropriate psychometric properties for the cultural, racial, or ethnic group of the individual in question. When counselors refer clients to other professionals for assessment, counselors provide specific referral questions and sufficient information about the client to help ensure that appropriate assessment instruments are utilized.

Common Dilemmas and Conflicts

- Counselors who select assessment instruments based on slick advertisements in publishers' catalogues may select assessment instruments that lack sufficient psychometric properties.
- Failure to closely scrutinize each assessment instrument's reliability, validity, and standardization may result in using instruments ill suited for specific clients and specific cultural groups.
- Counselors who fail to provide clear referral questions and relevant client data to third-party evaluators heighten the risk that inappropriate instruments will be used.
- Those who make vague assessment referrals such as "Do MMPI" or "Provide personality profile" run the risk of generating inadequate and unhelpful assessments.

Prevention and Positive Practice

✓ Prior to utilizing any assessment instruments, obtain the needed training in psychometrics so that instruments can be critically assessed for their appropriate use.

✓ Never use an assessment instrument without personally reviewing its psychometric properties and determining its appropriateness for the client in question.

✓ Put great thought into referrals for assessment, providing detailed information and specific referral questions.

✓ Always consider culture and other forms of diversity when reviewing the psychometric properties of an assessment instrument to ensure its appropriateness for a particular client.

E.7. Conditions of Assessment Administration *(See A.12.b, A.12.d.)*

E.7.a. Administration Conditions

Counselors administer assessments under the same conditions that were established in their standardization. When assessments are not administered under standard conditions, as may be necessary to accommodate clients with disabilities, or when unusual behavior or irregularities occur during the administration, those conditions are noted in interpretation, and the results may be designated as invalid or of questionable validity.

E.7.b. Technological Administration

Counselors ensure that administration programs function properly and provide clients with accurate results when technological or other electronic methods are used for assessment administration.

E.7.c. Unsupervised Assessments

Unless the assessment instrument is designed, intended, and validated for self-administration and/or -scoring, counselors do not permit inadequately supervised use.

E.7.d. Disclosure of Favorable Conditions

Prior to administration of assessments, conditions that produce most favorable assessment results are made known to the examinee.

Essential Elements

When conducting assessments of clients, counselors strive to administer all instruments in a standardized manner as prescribed in each instrument's manual. However, modifications may be made in administration to accommodate clients with disabilities or as the result of circumstances that arise during the assessment. When nonstandardized administration occurs, the details of protocol modifications are fully described in the report of the assessment. If deviation from standardized procedures may affect the validity of the assessment, this must be discussed specifically in the report. When utilizing technology such as computers to administer assessment instruments, counselors first confirm their proper functioning and ensure clients understand how to use them. Assessment instruments should only be used under the counselor's direct supervision unless the instrument is designed for take-home use, such as with many questionnaires and rating forms. Counselors provide clients with sufficient information about assessment procedures and ideal conditions for assessment prior to the evaluation to ensure the client's adequate preparation. Examples include ensuring clients are well rested, have eaten, and are not ill when the assessment is conducted.

Common Dilemmas and Conflicts

- Counselors who are careless about standardization procedures risk creating assessment administration conditions that invalidate the results.
- Failure to incorporate deviations from standardized procedures in the interpretation of results may lead to erroneous and harmful interpretations and recommendations.
- Assuming that clients are familiar with the use of technologies used to administer tests may lead to invalid results when clients use the technologies incorrectly.
- Counselors who are too busy and fail to directly supervise administration of assessment instruments heighten the risk of invalid assessment results.
- Failure to instruct clients about how to prepare for participation in an assessment may result in conditions that adversely affect client functioning and thus the value of the results.

Prevention and Positive Practice

✓ Always try to administer assessment instruments under the same conditions on which they were normed.

✓ When making needed accommodations for clients so they may participate in an assessment, always address the accommodations in your report and describe the potential impact on the validity of the results.

✓ Before using technologies such as computers to administer assessment instruments, always check for their smooth functioning first and ensure the client understands their use.

✓ Always orient clients to the assessment process in advance to help ensure their unencumbered participation and maximal performance.

✓ Appropriately supervise the administration of all assessment instruments unless they are designed for self-administration.

E.8. Multicultural Issues/Diversity in Assessment

> Counselors use with caution assessment techniques that were normed on populations other than that of the client. Counselors recognize the effects of age, color, culture, disability, ethnic group, gender, race, language preference, religion, spirituality, sexual orientation, and socioeconomic status on test administration and interpretation, and place test results in proper perspective with other relevant factors. *(See A.2.c., E.5.b.)*

Essential Elements

Counselors always strive to be sensitive to the role of diversity in the assessment process. When it is not possible to use assessment instruments that are appropriately normed for the client in question, counselors exercise appropriate caution. In these circumstances, counselors carefully attend to the potential impact diversity factors may have on the client's performance on the assessment instrument and fully address these concerns and limitations in their interpretation in the report.

Common Dilemmas and Conflicts

- Counselors who lack multicultural competence may overlook the role and impact of diversity factors on a client's functioning during an assessment.
- Counselors who fail to closely examine the psychometric properties of an assessment instrument—including the populations on which it was normed—risk using assessment instruments inappropriately.
- Counselors who fail to consider the full range of diversity variables may overlook less prominent aspects of culture that may nonetheless affect a client's assessment results.

Prevention and Positive Practice

✓ Carefully consider the potential impact of diversity factors—such as age, color, culture, disability, ethnic group, gender, race, language preference, religion, spirituality, sexual orientation, and socioeconomic status—on the client's functioning and assessment performance.

✓ Select assessment instruments with caution; when an instrument has not been normed on a salient aspect of the client's culture or identity, use the instrument cautiously.

✓ Always address the role of diversity factors on the administration, results, interpretation, and conclusions in your report.

E.9. Scoring and Interpretation of Assessments

E.9.a. Reporting

In reporting assessment results, counselors indicate reservations that exist regarding validity or reliability due to circumstances of the assessment or the inappropriateness of the norms for the person tested.

E.9.b. Research Instruments

Counselors exercise caution when interpreting the results of research instruments not having sufficient technical data to support respondent results. The specific purposes for the use of such instruments are stated explicitly to the examinee.

E.9.c. Assessment Services

Counselors who provide assessment scoring and interpretation services to support the assessment process confirm the validity of such interpretations. They accurately describe the purpose, norms, validity, reliability, and applications of the procedures and any special qualifications applicable to their use. The public offering of an automated test interpretation service is considered a professional-to-professional consultation. The formal responsibility of the consultant is to the consultee, but the ultimate and overriding responsibility is to the client. *(See D.2.)*

Essential Elements

When reporting assessment results, counselors always include statements that address any reservations about the appropriateness of the assessment instrument and any limitations to the interpretation or use of the results. Should a research instrument be used in an assessment, counselors take extra care to ensure the appropriateness of interpretations and conclusions drawn. Clients are always informed in advance of the experimental nature of the instrument and the rationale for using it. When providing assessment scoring and interpretation services, counselors fully and accurately describe these services so that potential users may carefully appraise the validity and usefulness of such services. Any potential limitations of these services or special requirements for their use should be disclosed in advance. Counselors who develop and provide assessment scoring and interpretation services take seriously their ethical obligations to both the professionals who use these services and the clients whom they assess.

Common Dilemmas and Conflicts

- Overlooking problematic assessment circumstances or norming inadequacies may contribute to erroneous interpretations of assessment results.
- Counselors who are eager to validate and norm a new instrument may be tempted to minimize the experimental nature of the instrument and fail to provide clients with adequate information about the purpose and limitations of the instrument.
- Financial motivations may compel a counselor to aggressively market assessment scoring and interpretation services without carefully explaining the valid uses and limitations of such services.

Prevention and Positive Practice

✓ Always pay careful attention to the circumstances in which assessment instruments are administered; abide by standardized administration protocols.

✓ In written assessment reports, clearly address the potential impact of all factors that may affect the reliability and validity of the assessment.

✓ When using assessment instruments that have not yet been fully validated, exercise great caution in their interpretation and fully explain potential limitations during the informed consent process.

✓ When offering counselors and other professionals assessment scoring and interpretation services, first provide them with all relevant information about reliability, validity, appropriate use, and limitations so they may make an informed decision about these services.

✓ Always keep in mind your ultimate ethical obligations to the users of assessment scoring and interpretation services, the clients being assessed.

E.10. Assessment Security

Counselors maintain the integrity and security of tests and other assessment techniques consistent with legal and contractual obligations. Counselors do not appropriate, reproduce, or modify published assessments or parts thereof without acknowledgment and permission from the publisher.

Essential Elements

Assessment instruments may be compromised and eventually rendered invalid if their content is inappropriately released or shared. Clients who have advance exposure to test items or unfair preparation for an assessment likely will generate results that are of limited value. Counselors should follow copyright laws and never photocopy or otherwise reproduce assessment materials, including response forms, without the written permission of the assessment publisher.

Common Dilemmas and Conflicts

- Counselors who are lax about assessment instrument security risk invalidating these measures.
- Counselors seeking to minimize expenses may be tempted to photocopy assessment materials in violation of copyright law.

Prevention and Positive Practice

✓ Carefully review user obligations and copyright restrictions each time you purchase or use a new assessment instrument.
✓ Always store assessment materials securely and restrict access only to appropriately trained individuals.
✓ Never release assessment materials that contain test items and their responses.
✓ Never photocopy assessment materials in an attempt to reduce expenses, unless the test publisher grants permission for such duplication.

E.11. Obsolete Assessments and Outdated Results

> Counselors do not use data or results from assessments that are obsolete or outdated for the current purpose. Counselors make every effort to prevent the misuse of obsolete measures and assessment data by others.

Essential Elements

Periodically, assessment instruments are updated and new editions are published. This is typically done to improve the value and relevance of the instrument over time as the population changes and as the profession learns more about how to assess clients effectively. Counselors avoid using obsolete assessment instruments and, whenever possible, use the most recent version of standardized instruments. Counselors similarly accept the obligation to educate colleagues, institutions, and the courts about this requirement as a way to ensure that others do not use obsolete assessment instruments or assessment data.

Common Dilemmas and Conflicts

- Counselors who are struggling financially may be tempted to use out-of-date assessment techniques when more appropriate or updated instruments are available.
- Counselors who are pressed for time may rely on outdated assessment results when evaluating or counseling a client, leading to potential harm.
- Counselors who are uncomfortable with confrontation may overlook the use of obsolete assessment techniques or data by others.

Prevention and Positive Practice

- ✓ Never use an obsolete or out-of-date assessment technique when an updated and improved version is available.
- ✓ When unsure about the validity or counseling value of a specific instrument, consult with a colleague who has expertise in assessment.
- ✓ Rather than make assessment and treatment decisions for clients based on obsolete data, conduct a new evaluation to ensure the validity and relevance of the data being used.
- ✓ Take responsibility to ensure that colleagues, supervisees, and subordinates only use the most recent and up-to-date assessment techniques and data.

E.12. Assessment Construction

> Counselors use established scientific procedures, relevant standards, and current professional knowledge for assessment design in the development, publication, and utilization of educational and psychological assessment techniques.

Essential Elements

Counselors may design and develop assessment techniques and instruments for use with specific client populations and assessment areas. When designing and constructing new assessment techniques, counselors rely on the most up-to-date scientific data and professional knowledge available to guide them. When appropriate, counselors use research and psychometric consultants to assist with this process. Counselors also conform to relevant professional standards in the publication of their new assessment instruments and in how they are used and applied.

Common Dilemmas and Conflicts

- Counselors motivated by quick financial gain may take shortcuts and overlook important steps in the development and validation of a new assessment technique.
- Counselors who are unfamiliar with prevailing test-development practices and standards and who fail to secure expert consultation in this area may be at risk of violating this ethical requirement.

Prevention and Positive Practice

- ✓ Before developing assessment procedures, first educate yourself on prevailing scientific professional standards.
- ✓ Meticulously follow these standards in all aspects of the development process.
- ✓ If you lack personal expertise with psychometrics and test development, seek appropriate consultation and assistance.
- ✓ When publishing new assessment techniques and instruments, carefully follow professional and ethical guidelines.

E.13. Forensic Evaluation: Evaluation for Legal Proceedings

E.13.a. Primary Obligations

When providing forensic evaluations, the primary obligation of counselors is to produce objective findings that can be substantiated based on information and techniques appropriate to the evaluation, which may include examination of the individual and/or review of records. Counselors are entitled to form professional opinions based on their professional knowledge and expertise that can be supported by the data gathered in evaluations. Counselors will define the limits of their reports or testimony, especially when an examination of the individual has not been conducted.

E.13.b. Consent for Evaluation

Individuals being evaluated are informed in writing that the relationship is for the purposes of an evaluation and is not counseling in nature, and entities or individuals who will receive the evaluation report are identified. Written consent to be evaluated is obtained from those being evaluated unless a court orders evaluations to be conducted without the written consent of individuals being evaluated. When children or vulnerable adults are being evaluated, informed written consent is obtained from a parent or guardian.

E.13.c. Client Evaluation Prohibited

Counselors do not evaluate for forensic purposes individuals they currently counsel or individuals they have counseled in the past. Counselors do not accept as counseling clients for forensic purposes individuals they are evaluating or individuals they have evaluated in the past.

E.13.d. Avoid Potentially Harmful Relationships

Counselors who provide forensic evaluations avoid potentially harmful professional or personal relationships with family members, romantic partners, and close friends of individuals they are evaluating or have evaluated in the past.

Essential Elements

Appropriately trained counselors may provide a great service by conducting assessments for forensic purposes. Counselors functioning in forensic roles must be familiar with the unique obligations and objectives of forensic work; they base their assessment findings on appropriate techniques and sufficient data to support statements and recommendations. Counselors are cautious about making statements about individuals they have not evaluated personally and clarify all limits to the data on which they base their conclusions. Counselors ensure that all clients provide fully informed consent that addresses the purposes of the evaluation and potential uses of data, results, and interpretations. When an individual is unable to provide consent, counselors obtain informed consent from a suitable individual such as a parent or guardian. When an evaluation is court ordered, counselors endeavor to share all relevant information about the evaluation and its purposes with clients even though clients may not provide informed consent. Counselors avoid potentially harmful or exploitative relationships that could adversely impact their objectivity, such as conducting a forensic evaluation of a current counseling client or others with whom they have a close or personal relationship.

Common Dilemmas and Conflicts

- Counselors unfamiliar with the nature and demands of forensic evaluations may be ill prepared to function ethically and competently in forensic roles.
- Counselors who assume that clients understand the parameters and potential uses of a forensic evaluation may end up violating clients' rights and practicing unethically.
- Counselors who overestimate their ability to maintain objectivity when conducting a forensic evaluation and providing testimony about an individual with whom they have a close or personal relationship risk bringing harm to that individual and violating this *Code of Ethics.*

Prevention and Positive Practice

✓ Before providing any forensic service, obtain the training and supervised experience necessary to conduct forensic evaluations competently.
✓ Ensure that all individuals evaluated in conjunction with a forensic matter first provide fully informed voluntary consent.
✓ Take special care to protect the rights of those who are unable to provide informed consent themselves.
✓ Only make statements in court that are supported by available data, and be extremely cautious in making statements about individuals you have not personally assessed.
✓ Always clarify the limits of forensic data and interpretations.
✓ Whenever possible, avoid conducting a forensic evaluation of or provide expert witness testimony about an individual who is a client or with whom you have a close personal relationship.

Section F

Supervision, Training, and Teaching

Introduction

Counselors aspire to foster meaningful and respectful professional relationships and to maintain appropriate boundaries with supervisees and students. Counselors have theoretical and pedagogical foundations for their work and aim to be fair, accurate, and honest in their assessments of counselors-in-training.

F.1. Counselor Supervision and Client Welfare

F.1.a. Client Welfare

A primary obligation of counseling supervisors is to monitor the services provided by other counselors or counselors-in-training. Counseling supervisors monitor client welfare and supervisee clinical performance and professional development. To fulfill these obligations, supervisors meet regularly with supervisees to review case notes, samples of clinical work, or live observations. Supervisees have a responsibility to understand and follow the *ACA Code of Ethics*.

Essential Elements

Some of the most important roles occupied by counselors are those of trainer and supervisor. In their supervisory roles, counselors assist counselors-in-training to develop the needed education, skills, experience, and values to be effective and competent counselors. When they contribute to the professional development of trainees, counselors should base their training and supervision on established theoretical perspectives and evidence-based supervisory practices. Counselors must provide appropriate active oversight of supervisees and trainees to ensure their optimal professional development as well as to ensure the welfare of those receiving counseling services; supervisors are first and foremost committed to ensuring the safety and best interests of clients. Counselor supervisors follow the *ACA Code of Ethics* and ensure that their trainees do so as well.

Common Dilemmas and Conflicts

- Counselors for whom supervision of trainees is an added employment responsibility may view this as a burden and overlook their responsibilities to supervisees and their clients.
- Counselors who fail to assess supervisees' training needs may overestimate their abilities and underestimate their need for oversight.
- Counselors without specific training in supervision may lack needed competencies and be at risk for harming trainees and their clients.

Prevention and Positive Practice

✓ Only provide supervision after obtaining the needed education and training to ensure competence in this role and only if you can offer sufficient time and appropriate oversight.
✓ Assess each supervisee's competencies and training needs at the outset of the relationship to help determine the intensity of supervision and level of oversight needed.
✓ Treat all supervisees with respect, as colleagues-in-training.
✓ Actively promote ethical practice by supervisees through attention to ethics issues in ongoing supervision sessions and through professional role modeling.
✓ Carefully abide by laws and licensure regulations regarding counselor supervision.

F.1.b. Counselor Credentials

Counseling supervisors work to ensure that clients are aware of the qualifications of the supervisees who render services to the clients. *(See A.2.b.)*

F.1.c. Informed Consent and Client Rights

Supervisors make supervisees aware of client rights including the protection of client privacy and confidentiality in the counseling relationship. Supervisees provide clients with professional disclosure information and inform them of how the supervision process influences the limits of confidentiality. Supervisees make clients aware of who will have access to records of the counseling relationship and how these records will be used. *(See A.2.b., B.1.d.)*

Essential Elements

Counselors-in-training only provide counseling services under the direct supervision of an appropriately trained and credentialed counselor or allied mental health professional, depending on the requirements of local credentialing laws and regulations. Supervisors ensure that trainees provide all clients with voluntary informed consent prior to providing counseling services. Clients are informed that the supervisee is a counselor-in-training and that the services are being provided under the direct oversight of the supervisor. Additionally, clients are fully informed that all counseling information will be shared with the supervisor. Finally, supervisees explain confidentiality policies and procedures to clients.

Common Dilemmas and Conflicts

- Counselors who fail to provide sufficient oversight for supervisees may fail to protect client rights.
- Failure to fully address supervision and confidentiality issues in the informed consent process may result in ethics violations and harm to clients.

Prevention and Positive Practice

✓ Always ensure that an informed consent process is carried out by supervisees with each client before any counseling services are provided.
✓ Thoroughly review with clients the supervisor's role, access to counseling information, and all limits to confidentiality at the outset.
✓ Ensure that supervisees accurately disclose their credentials, qualifications, and trainee status to clients.

F.2. Counselor Supervision Competence

F.2.a. Supervisor Preparation

Prior to offering clinical supervision services, counselors are trained in supervision methods and techniques. Counselors who offer clinical supervision services regularly pursue continuing education activities including both counseling and supervision topics and skills. *(See C.2.a., C.2.f.)*

F.2.b. Multicultural Issues/Diversity in Supervision

Counseling supervisors are aware of and address the role of multiculturalism/diversity in the supervisory relationship.

Essential Elements

Before a counselor undertakes supervision of a counselor-in-training, he or she must ensure competence both in the practice of supervision and in the area of counseling being supervised (e.g., assessment, family counseling, counseling persons with eating disorders). Counselor supervisors develop and maintain their knowledge and skills in both areas through ongoing education, training, and other professional development activities. Additionally, counselor supervisors are multiculturally competent; they integrate attention to all relevant aspects of diversity in their supervision of counseling trainees.

Common Dilemmas and Conflicts

- Counselors who are new to the practice of supervision may fail to ensure their own competence to supervise before embarking on this role.

- Counselors who engage primarily in counseling services may overlook the fact that the ethical practice of counselor supervision requires unique competencies.
- Supervisors lacking an awareness of and sensitivity to diversity issues may cause harm to supervisees and the clients they counsel.

Prevention and Positive Practice

✓ Always obtain specific training in counseling supervision before providing any supervision services.
✓ Actively seek out ongoing continuing education and professional development activities in your areas of counseling expertise and in the practice of counseling supervision.
✓ Remember that competent supervision requires competence as both a supervisor and a counselor.
✓ Be vigilant to multicultural and other diversity issues in your supervision relationships and help supervisees to process diversity concerns with clients.

F.3. Supervisory Relationships

F.3.a. Relationship Boundaries With Supervisees

Counseling supervisors clearly define and maintain ethical professional, personal, and social relationships with their supervisees. Counseling supervisors avoid nonprofessional relationships with current supervisees. If supervisors must assume other professional roles (e.g., clinical and administrative supervisor, instructor) with supervisees, they work to minimize potential conflicts and explain to supervisees the expectations and responsibilities associated with each role. They do not engage in any form of nonprofessional interaction that may compromise the supervisory relationship.

F.3.b. Sexual Relationships

Sexual or romantic interactions or relationships with current supervisees are prohibited.

F.3.c. Sexual Harassment

Counseling supervisors do not condone or subject supervisees to sexual harassment. *(See C.6.a.)*

F.3.d. Close Relatives and Friends

Counseling supervisors avoid accepting close relatives, romantic partners, or friends as supervisees.

F.3.e. Potentially Beneficial Relationships

Counseling supervisors are aware of the power differential in their relationships with supervisees. If they believe nonprofessional relationships with a supervisee may be potentially beneficial to the supervisee, they take precautions similar to those taken by counselors when working with clients. Examples of potentially beneficial interactions or relationships include attending a formal ceremony; hospital visits; providing support during a stressful event; or mutual membership in a professional association, organization, or community. Counseling supervisors engage in open discussions with supervisees when they consider entering into relationships with them outside of their roles as clinical and/or administrative supervisors. Before engaging in nonprofessional relationships, supervisors discuss with supervisees and document the rationale for such interactions, potential benefits or drawbacks, and anticipated consequences for the supervisee. Supervisors clarify the specific nature and limitations of the additional role(s) they will have with the supervisee.

Essential Elements

Supervisors should never abuse the power and influence they always hold in relation to supervisees. Although it is neither possible nor desirable to avoid all multiple relationships with supervisees, supervisors should avoid any nonprofessional relationship with supervisees that is likely to impair objectivity or harm the supervisee. Before engaging in a potentially appropriate secondary role with a supervisee—as often occurs in educational, training, and small community settings—counselors openly discuss any implications of the extra relationship with the supervisee, and they only embark on the extraprofessional relationship if it is not likely to be harmful to the supervisee or to the supervision relationship. Multiple relationships with others who are closely associated with the supervisee should be considered with equal caution. Counselors never engage in sexual relationships with supervisees or those closely associated with supervisees because of the great likelihood of harm or abuse of power and the likely distortion of the supervisor's objectivity and judgment. Additionally, counselor supervisors should never engage in, tolerate, or condone sexual harassment of supervisees.

Common Dilemmas and Conflicts

- Supervisors working in small training centers or communities often find multiple relationships with supervisees to be more prevalent.
- Supervisors experiencing stress and distress in their personal or professional lives, and who are not receiving needed assistance, may be at elevated risk for inappropriate multiple relationships with supervisees.
- Supervisors who overestimate their ability to juggle multiple roles and minimize the dangers to supervisees may be at risk for entering exploitive relationships with supervisees.

Prevention and Positive Practice

✓ Carefully consider all multiple relationships from the perspective of the supervisee.

✓ Always make multiple relationship decisions with the supervisee's best interests in mind.

✓ When experiencing distress, loneliness, or difficulties in your life, seek professional assistance and do not attempt to get personal needs met through relationships with supervisees.

- ✓ Always treat supervisees with respect, and never engage in sexual harassment.
- ✓ When considering entering a multiple relationship with a supervisee or a person closely associated with the supervisee, consider options, alternatives, and the potential impact on your objectivity and judgment.
- ✓ If a nonprofessional relationship with a supervisee may be neutral or beneficial, be sure to discuss the pros and cons of the extra relationship with your supervisee before moving ahead.
- ✓ Sexual intimacies with a supervisee are always unethical.

F.4. Supervisor Responsibilities

F.4.a. Informed Consent for Supervision

Supervisors are responsible for incorporating into their supervision the principles of informed consent and participation. Supervisors inform supervisees of the policies and procedures to which they are to adhere and the mechanisms for due process appeal of individual supervisory actions.

F.4.b. Emergencies and Absences

Supervisors establish and communicate to supervisees procedures for contacting them or, in their absence, alternative on-call supervisors to assist in handling crises.

F.4.c. Standards for Supervisees

Supervisors make their supervisees aware of professional and ethical standards and legal responsibilities. Supervisors of postdegree counselors encourage these counselors to adhere to professional standards of practice. *(See C.1.)*

F.4.d. Termination of the Supervisory Relationship

Supervisors or supervisees have the right to terminate the supervisory relationship with adequate notice. Reasons for withdrawal are provided to the other party. When cultural, clinical, or professional issues are crucial to the viability of the supervisory relationship, both parties make efforts to resolve differences. When termination is warranted, supervisors make appropriate referrals to possible alternative supervisors.

Essential Elements

Just as with any other professional relationship, counselors begin the supervision relationship with an informed consent process to ensure that the supervisee enters the relationship informed regarding expectations and role requirements. Supervisors should carefully explain all relevant policies, procedures, responsibilities, and expectations so that both supervisor and supervisee are in agreement with regard to each and so that supervisees can effectively communicate them to clients as appropriate. Supervisors provide supervisees with emergency contact information and carefully review procedures for handling crises and emergencies in their absence or when they are unavailable. Supervisors are wise to use a written supervisory contract so that key elements of this informed consent process are committed to writing and clearly endorsed by both parties at the outset of the relationship. As professional role models, supervisors model ethical behavior that adheres to professional standards and communicate the same expectations of supervisees. When either party is dissatisfied with the supervisory relationship, they first attempt to resolve it collaboratively through open discussion. If this proves ineffective and the relationship is terminated, the supervisor offers appropriate referrals to other supervisors.

Common Dilemmas and Conflicts

- Failure to engage in a thorough informed consent process at the beginning of the supervision relationship may result in conflicts, dissatisfaction, and failed expectations for the supervisor and supervisee alike.
- Supervisors who do not make advance arrangements for coverage during periods of absence may leave supervisees and their clients poorly served and at risk of harm.
- Supervisors who experience conflicts or dissatisfaction with supervisees may be at risk of abandoning them and terminating supervision without due process.

Prevention and Positive Practice

✓ Provide a thorough informed consent process to every supervisee at the outset of the relationship.
✓ Always include all roles, responsibilities, expectations, emergency coverage, and contact information in the informed consent. Update whenever changes arise.
✓ Be sure that supervisees understand due process procedures and appropriate channels for formally protesting or challenging supervisory decisions or evaluations.
✓ Consider using a written supervision contract so that mutual expectations and supervisor policies are clearly agreed upon at the outset of supervision.
✓ Integrate a focus on ethical practice and adherence to prevailing professional standards into all aspects of the supervision process.
✓ Whenever supervision must end, openly discuss the relevant issues and make referrals to other appropriately trained supervisors.
✓ When conflicts with supervisees or termination of supervision occurs with some frequency, seek consultation and honestly explore your own contribution to supervision failures.

F.5. Counseling Supervision Evaluation, Remediation, and Endorsement

F.5.a. Evaluation

Supervisors document and provide supervisees with ongoing performance appraisal and evaluation feedback and schedule periodic formal evaluative sessions throughout the supervisory relationship.

F.5.b. Limitations

Through ongoing evaluation and appraisal, supervisors are aware of the limitations of supervisees that might impede performance. Supervisors assist supervisees in securing remedial assistance when needed. They recommend dismissal from training programs, applied counseling settings, or state or voluntary professional credentialing processes when those supervisees are unable to provide competent professional services. Supervisors seek consultation and document their decisions to dismiss or refer supervisees for assistance. They ensure that supervisees are aware of options available to them to address such decisions. *(See C.2.g.)*

F.5.c. Counseling for Supervisees

If supervisees request counseling, supervisors provide them with acceptable referrals. Counselors do not provide counseling services to supervisees. Supervisors address interpersonal competencies in terms of the impact of these issues on clients, the supervisory relationship, and professional functioning. *(See F.3.a.)*

F.5.d. Endorsement

Supervisors endorse supervisees for certification, licensure, employment, or completion of an academic or training program only when they believe supervisees are qualified for the endorsement. Regardless of qualifications, supervisors do not endorse supervisees whom they believe to be impaired in any way that would interfere with the performance of the duties associated with the endorsement.

Essential Elements

In addition to providing training and oversight, supervisors provide an evaluative function for most supervisees. Supervisors provide supervisees with timely verbal and written feedback on all aspects of their performance and professional functioning, make suggestions for any needed remediation, and provide opportunities for this remediation. If supervisees are not able to meet standards and expectations, supervisors have a responsibility to the counseling profession and the clients they serve to recommend appropriate remediation or dismissal from a training program if needed. Should a supervisee require personal counseling, the supervisor recommends this and assists with the referral process. However, supervisors never provide counseling for supervisees themselves because of the inappropriate dual relationship this would create *(see A.5.a, F.3.a.)*. Supervisors only provide their endorsement of a supervisee for licensure, certification, employment, or completion of degree requirements when the supervisee has met all relevant requirements and is competent to function as a counselor.

Common Dilemmas and Conflicts

- Supervisors who fail to make accurate evaluation and feedback a routine part of supervision may fail to identify and address problems of professional competence in a timely manner.

- Supervisors who are uncomfortable with evaluating others and providing negative feedback may be at risk of perpetuating professional incompetence in supervisees.
- Discomfort with confrontation and anticipated conflict may result in endorsing supervisees who are ill prepared for credentialing and independent practice in counseling.
- Supervisors who provide counseling to their supervisees risk impaired objectivity and judgment, and harm to their supervisees.

Prevention and Positive Practice

✓ Include a structured evaluation process in the informed consent agreement and provide each supervisee with feedback—verbal and written—on a regular basis.

✓ Provide supervisees with recommendations for remediation of all areas of deficiency.

✓ Attend to each supervisee's emotional and interpersonal functioning and recommend personal counseling when needed.

✓ Never provide personal counseling to supervisees but make appropriate referrals as needed.

✓ Clarify expectations with training programs up front, provide them with ongoing feedback on supervisees, and recommend dismissal from the program when remediation efforts are not effective.

✓ Only endorse supervisees who possess the needed competence to practice effectively. Never endorse supervisees who have impaired professional competence.

✓ Guard against inflation and inaccuracy when writing letters of recommendation for supervisees.

F.6. Responsibilities of Counselor Educators

F.6.a. Counselor Educators

Counselor educators who are responsible for developing, implementing, and supervising educational programs are skilled as teachers and practitioners. They are knowledgeable regarding the ethical, legal, and regulatory aspects of the profession, are skilled in applying that knowledge, and make students and supervisees aware of their responsibilities. Counselor educators conduct counselor education and training programs in an ethical manner and serve as role models for professional behavior. *(See C.1., C.2.a., C.2.c.)*

F.6.b. Infusing Multicultural Issues/Diversity

Counselor educators infuse material related to multiculturalism/diversity into all courses and workshops for the development of professional counselors.

F.6.c. Integration of Study and Practice

Counselor educators establish education and training programs that integrate academic study and supervised practice.

F.6.d. Teaching Ethics

Counselor educators make students and supervisees aware of the ethical responsibilities and standards of the profession and the ethical responsibilities of students to the profession. Counselor educators infuse ethical considerations throughout the curriculum. *(See C.1.)*

Essential Elements

Assisting with the education of those training to become counselors is an important professional role for counselors. Counselors working as educators ensure they have the needed competence—both as subject matter experts and as teachers—before accepting education roles. They remain current on relevant ethical, legal, and regulatory aspects of the counseling profession and instill the importance of these elements in their education efforts. Counselor educators see themselves as professional role models; they therefore maintain the highest standards of practice and conduct in their interactions with students. Multicultural issues and diversity are integrated into all aspects of teaching, and counselors emphasize their importance to students through teaching and interpersonal behavior. Recognizing that genuine competence requires the integration of education and applied practice, counselor educators integrate supervised counseling experience with classroom learning experiences.

Common Dilemmas and Conflicts

- Counselor educators with a myopic view of their teaching role and responsibilities may fail to infuse multiculturalism, diversity, and ethics into their teaching.
- Overlooking one's responsibilities as a professional role model for students may result in engaging in unethical practices that undermine ethics education efforts.
- Counselor educators who are competent in the area of counseling they are teaching but who fail to develop and maintain competence in teaching strategies and methods risk engaging in incompetent counselor education.

Prevention and Positive Practice

✓ Obtain training in effective teaching practices prior to entering the teaching role and then maintain and enhance these skills over time.

✓ Remain current on ethical, legal, and regulatory issues in counseling and integrate them into all of the courses you teach.

✓ Emphasize through your teaching the importance of cultural competence and attention to diversity issues in all aspects of counseling.

✓ In your interactions with students, remain cognizant of your responsibilities as one of their primary professional role models.

✓ Ensure that your counselor training program integrates didactic instruction with supervised counseling experiences to optimally develop students' counseling competence.

F.6.e. Peer Relationships

Counselor educators make every effort to ensure that the rights of peers are not compromised when students or supervisees lead counseling groups or provide clinical supervision. Counselor educators take steps to ensure that students and supervisees understand they have the same ethical obligations as counselor educators, trainers, and supervisors.

F.6.f. Innovative Theories and Techniques

When counselor educators teach counseling techniques/procedures that are innovative, without an empirical foundation, or without a well-grounded theoretical foundation, they define the counseling techniques/procedures as "unproven" or "developing" and explain to students the potential risks and ethical considerations of using such techniques/procedures.

F.6.g. Field Placements

Counselor educators develop clear policies within their training programs regarding field placement and other clinical experiences. Counselor educators provide clearly stated roles and responsibilities for the student or supervisee, the site supervisor, and the program supervisor. They confirm that site supervisors are qualified to provide supervision and inform site supervisors of their professional and ethical responsibilities in this role.

F.6.h. Professional Disclosure

Before initiating counseling services, counselors-in-training disclose their status as students and explain how this status affects the limits of confidentiality. Counselor educators ensure that the clients at field placements are aware of the services rendered and the qualifications of the students and supervisees rendering those services. Students and supervisees obtain client permission before they use any information concerning the counseling relationship in the training process. *(See A.2.b.)*

Essential Elements

When educating students, counselors frequently provide them with supervised counseling experiences. In these situations students must understand their ethical responsibilities and must follow all aspects of the *ACA Code of Ethics*. Counselors are careful to provide appropriate instruction and oversight to ensure that others are not harmed. For instance, they work to safeguard the rights of peers when counselors-in-training lead groups or provide supervision. When teaching innovative or novel techniques that are not yet supported by empirical findings, counselors present them clearly as unproven and do not imply that they are evidence based or well established. Because supervised clinical experience is an integral component of counselor education *(see F.6.c.)*, educators ensure that students at field placements are appropriately supervised, that they provide clients with informed consent before providing any counseling services, and that clients understand each student's training status and how being supervised affects the limits to confidentiality. Educators ensure that roles and responsibilities of program faculty, students, and site supervisors are clarified in advance of a student entering a field placement. All site supervisors must have the requisite experience and competence to provide supervision in the relevant areas of counseling practice. Finally, counselor educators clarify expectations regarding the professional and ethical responsibilities for supervisors before they meet with students.

Common Dilemmas and Conflicts

- Educators who overestimate students' abilities and who fail to supervise them closely heighten the risk of harm to those with whom students interact professionally.
- Educators who trust but fail to verify that field placement supervisors are competent and ethical increase the risk of poor training experiences and potential harm to students.
- Students who do not disclose their training status to clients risk violating clients' trust and harming the counseling relationship.
- Counselor educators who become enamored with a novel counseling approach may neglect to inform students and supervisees about the theoretical and empirical limitations of the approach.

Prevention and Positive Practice

✓ Carefully assess each student's level of experience and competence and then ensure the student receives the appropriate type and level of supervision.
✓ Instruct all students and supervisees about their professional and ethical obligations prior to clearing them for field placements. Review these obligations periodically.
✓ Always clarify roles, responsibilities, and expectations of site supervisors and educators prior to students entering the field placement.
✓ Ensure that supervisees fully inform all clients about their training status, the existence and role of supervision, and the relevant limits to confidentiality.
✓ When instructing students in the use of techniques that are not yet empirically supported, exercise caution and provide sufficient oversight to ensure the well-being of clients.
✓ Take steps to ensure that students and supervisees respect and safeguard the rights of peers.

F.7. Student Welfare

F.7.a. Orientation

Counselor educators recognize that orientation is a developmental process that continues throughout the educational and clinical training of students. Counseling faculty provide prospective students with information about the counselor education program's expectations:

1. the type and level of skill and knowledge acquisition required for successful completion of the training;

2. program training goals, objectives, and mission, and subject matter to be covered;
3. bases for evaluation;
4. training components that encourage self-growth or self-disclosure as part of the training process;
5. the type of supervision settings and requirements of the sites for required clinical field experiences;
6. student and supervisee evaluation and dismissal policies and procedures; and
7. up-to-date employment prospects for graduates.

F.7.b. Self-Growth Experiences

Counselor education programs delineate requirements for self-disclosure or self-growth experiences in their admission and program materials. Counselor educators use professional judgment when designing training experiences they conduct that require student and supervisee self-growth or self-disclosure. Students and supervisees are made aware of the ramifications their self-disclosure may have when counselors whose primary role as teacher, trainer, or supervisor requires acting on ethical obligations to the profession. Evaluative components of experiential training experiences explicitly delineate predetermined academic standards that are separate and do not depend on the student's level of self-disclosure. Counselor educators may require trainees to seek professional help to address any personal concerns that may be affecting their competency.

Essential Elements

Educators ensure that all program descriptions and promotional materials accurately reflect program requirements. They describe all relevant educational and counseling experiences, degree requirements, expectations, and evaluation and dismissal policies with prospective students in program descriptions. Additionally, counselor educators fully inform current students about all relevant expectations and all factors that may affect successful completion of the training program. If self-disclosure and personal growth experiences are part of a training program, counselors take time to help students understand how personal information shared through self-disclosure may be used by the training program, and how students will be evaluated in self-growth experiences. If self-disclosures and participation in self-growth experiences indicate issues likely to affect the student's competence as a counselor, the educator may require the student to receive professional help in order to remain in the training program. Finally, counselor educators avoid leading self-growth experiences themselves if these experiences have a counseling or psychotherapy flavor so as to avoid potentially uncomfortable or even harmful dual roles with students *(see F.5.c.)*.

Common Dilemmas and Conflicts

- Counselor educators who fail to adequately orient prospective and current students regarding expectations and evaluative processes heighten the risk of conflicts with ill-informed students.

- Educators who fail to grasp the inherent risks to students when self-disclosure and self-growth experiences are required may fail to secure appropriate informed consent for these experiences.
- Training programs that do not establish and communicate clear and structured evaluation procedures for student performance risk graduating or credentialing students who are incompetent or ill suited for the profession.
- Counselor educators who personally like certain students may be at risk of overlooking student difficulties and fail to require needed remediation or professional assistance.

Prevention and Positive Practice

✓ Always provide prospective students with a description of your training program's requirements, expectations, and standards, as well as how they will be evaluated.
✓ Be sure to provide each entering student with a thorough orientation wherein each of these requirements, expectations, and standards are reviewed.
✓ Include self-disclosure and self-growth requirements in program descriptions and ensure that all students understand these requirements and any alternatives.
✓ Create a structured evaluation process that includes careful monitoring of students' disclosures and interpersonal functioning; require remediation or professional assistance when indicated.
✓ Work hard to prevent personal feelings about or toward a student to interfere with taking needed actions such as requiring remediation, professional assistance, or even dismissal from the program.

F.8. Student Responsibilities

F.8.a. Standards for Students

Counselors-in-training have a responsibility to understand and follow the *ACA Code of Ethics* and adhere to applicable laws, regulatory policies, and rules and policies governing professional staff behavior at the agency or placement setting. Students have the same obligation to clients as those required of professional counselors. *(See C.1., H.1.)*

F.8.b. Impairment

Counselors-in-training refrain from offering or providing counseling services when their physical, mental, or emotional problems are likely to harm a client or others. They are alert to the signs of impairment, seek assistance for problems, and notify their program supervisors when they are aware that they are unable to effectively provide services. In addition, they seek appropriate professional services for themselves to remediate the problems that are interfering with their ability to provide services to others. *(See A.1., C.2.d., C.2.g.)*

Essential Elements

The *ACA Code of Ethics* applies to students and trainees just as it does to professional counselors. Students must familiarize themselves with and follow each aspect of this

Code of Ethics along with relevant policies, regulations, and laws. Students in each facility or setting where students provide counseling services adhere to site-specific policies and rules. Counseling students are alert to the signs of distress, burnout, and impaired professional competence. When present, they take needed corrective actions, including seeking professional assistance, notifying their supervisors of these concerns, and following supervisors' recommendations. To prevent these difficulties from impairing their competence, students monitor their personal and professional functioning on an ongoing basis, seek appropriate supervision, and engage in ongoing self-care.

Common Dilemmas and Conflicts

- Students who assume that ethical, legal, and regulatory requirements of practicing counselors do not apply to them risk engaging in a wide range of harmful and inappropriate behaviors.
- Students who attend to the *ACA Code of Ethics* but who overlook or remain unfamiliar with laws, regulations, and rules relevant to their placement or work setting may be at risk of jeopardizing their trainee status and inadvertently harming clients.
- Counselor trainees who fail to monitor personal and professional functioning, overlook signs of distress and burnout, and ignore the effects of life stresses risk developing impaired professional competence and harming both clients and the profession.
- Students who fail to notify supervisors about distress and signs of impaired functioning risk further degradation of performance and competence.

Prevention and Positive Practice

✓ Each educator and supervisor should ensure that students understand and accept the need to follow the *ACA Code of Ethics* and relevant laws, regulations, and rules in all counseling roles.

✓ Students must accept the same ethical responsibilities as practicing professional counselors.

✓ Students and supervisees should closely monitor their personal and professional functioning and be alert to signs of distress and impairment.

✓ Share signs of impaired professional functioning with supervisors to facilitate needed corrective actions; in the supervision informed consent process with students, supervisors should be clear how this information will be handled and who in the training program will have access to it.

✓ Always practice good self-care, and never ignore or overlook signs of distress, burnout, or impairment.

F.9. Evaluation and Remediation of Students

F.9.a. Evaluation

Counselors clearly state to students, prior to and throughout the training program, the levels of competency expected, appraisal methods, and timing of evaluations for both didactic and clinical competencies. Counselor educators provide students with ongoing performance appraisal and evaluation feedback throughout the training program.

F.9.b. Limitations

Counselor educators, throughout ongoing evaluation and appraisal, are aware of and address the inability of some students to achieve counseling competencies that might impede performance. Counselor educators

1. assist students in securing remedial assistance when needed,
2. seek professional consultation and document their decision to dismiss or refer students for assistance, and
3. ensure that students have recourse in a timely manner to address decisions to require them to seek assistance or to dismiss them and provide students with due process according to institutional policies and procedures. *(See C.2.g.)*

F.9.c. Counseling for Students

If students request counseling or if counseling services are required as part of a remediation process, counselor educators provide acceptable referrals.

Essential Elements

The education and training of counselors requires ongoing assessment of trainees to ensure they are achieving established standards and milestones of professional development. Counselor educators inform students of all relevant expectations and provide them with detailed feedback on an ongoing basis. When students fail to meet expectations, educators and supervisors make recommendations for remediation, help students to obtain needed assistance, and set timelines for meeting clear performance standards. Educators always afford students due process rights for challenging adverse decisions such as the requirement to repeat training experiences or dismissal from the training program. Supervisors fully document all actions and their rationale and make such documentation available for review. When counseling is a part of a student's remediation plan, educators make appropriate referrals but do not engage in such counseling themselves.

Common Dilemmas and Conflicts

- Counselors who fail to communicate and then follow established policies and procedures for student evaluation and feedback are acting unethically and may suffer administrative or legal action.
- Providing negative feedback without suggestions for remediation and improved functioning violates the spirit of this standard.
- Educators who expect students to obtain remediation or counseling on their own are neglecting their responsibility to assist students with this process.

Prevention and Positive Practice

✓ Share clearly with students and trainees all expectations, standards of performance, and competencies needed to successfully complete the program.

✓ Inform students of the methods and timing of evaluation and monitor students' performance on an ongoing basis.

- ✓ Provide informal feedback on a regular basis in between more formal evaluations.
- ✓ When students are not meeting stated expectations, develop a remediation plan and assist them to obtain needed help.
- ✓ Document carefully your rationale and process when you place a student on probation, require remediation, or dismiss a student from a program.

F.10. Roles and Relationships Between Counselor Educators and Students

F.10.a. Sexual or Romantic Relationships

Sexual or romantic interactions or relationships with current students are prohibited.

F.10.b. Sexual Harassment

Counselor educators do not condone or subject students to sexual harassment. *(See C.6.a.)*

F.10.c. Relationships With Former Students

Counselor educators are aware of the power differential in the relationship between faculty and students. Faculty members foster open discussions with former students when considering engaging in a social, sexual, or other intimate relationship. Faculty members discuss with the former student how their former relationship may affect the change in relationship.

F.10.d. Nonprofessional Relationships

Counselor educators avoid nonprofessional or ongoing professional relationships with students in which there is a risk of potential harm to the student or that may compromise the training experience or grades assigned. In addition, counselor educators do not accept any form of professional services, fees, commissions, reimbursement, or remuneration from a site for student or supervisee placement.

F.10.e. Counseling Services

Counselor educators do not serve as counselors to current students unless this is a brief role associated with a training experience.

F.10.f. Potentially Beneficial Relationships

Counselor educators are aware of the power differential in the relationship between faculty and students. If they believe a nonprofessional relationship with a student may be potentially beneficial to the student, they take precautions similar to those taken by counselors when working with clients. Examples of potentially beneficial interactions or relationships include, but are not limited to, attending a formal ceremony; hospital visits; providing support during a stressful event; or mutual membership in a professional association, organization,

> or community. Counselor educators engage in open discussions with students when they consider entering into relationships with students outside of their roles as teachers and supervisors. They discuss with students the rationale for such interactions, the potential benefits and drawbacks, and the anticipated consequences for the student. Educators clarify the specific nature and limitations of the additional role(s) they will have with the student prior to engaging in a nonprofessional relationship. Nonprofessional relationships with students should be time-limited and initiated with student consent.

Essential Elements

As is true in their relationships with clients, an imbalance of power exists between faculty and their students. Accordingly, counselor educators never engage in sexual or romantic relationships with current students and are very cautious about entering such relationships with former students because of the potential for impaired objectivity, exploitation, and harm to the former student. Similarly, counselor educators do not provide counseling services to students (unless as part of a brief training experience) because of the high potential for impaired objectivity and possible harm. Counselor educators never sexually harass students and avoid all relationships with students that might reasonably be expected to result in harm. Yet, some extra roles with students may not be contraindicated. In these cases, counselors first openly discuss relevant relationship dynamics, risks, and benefits with the student; clarify roles and expectations; and then remain vigilant for signs of possible harm. Incidental contacts, such as in the local community and in professional organizations, are not necessarily harmful. However, in all multiple relationship situations, available options and alternatives should be considered along with anticipated risks and benefits; as the power holder in relationships with students, the counselor educator retains primary ethical responsibility for avoiding potentially harmful nonprofessional roles.

Common Dilemmas and Conflicts

- Educators who work closely with students may develop strong feelings of attraction and be tempted to engage in social or romantic relationships with them.
- Educators who fail to appreciate their power over students are at risk of entering a harmful and exploitative relationship.
- An educator who commences a social or romantic relationship with a former student without thoughtful consideration and discussion of the potential dangers is at risk of harming the former student.
- Attempts at strict avoidance of all nonprofessional relationships place counselors in an untenable situation and diminish opportunities for appropriate and helpful relationships with students.
- Educators who add business, social, or other relationships to a supervisory or educative relationship with a student place themselves at risk in this area.

Prevention and Positive Practice

✓ Know established ethics standards, and be mindful of the power and influence you hold over students.

- ✓ Never enter potentially harmful or exploitative multiple relationships with students.
- ✓ Never have a sexual relationship with a student or supervisee.
- ✓ Be careful to avoid humor, comments, or other behaviors that might be construed by students as harassing.
- ✓ Use a decision-making process to consider potential risks and benefits, reasonably available options and alternatives, and the student's best interests before entering into a nonprofessional relationship with a student.
- ✓ With the exception of brief course-related educational experiences, never serve simultaneously as a student's faculty member and counselor.

F.11. Multicultural/Diversity Competence in Counselor Education and Training Programs

F.11.a. Faculty Diversity

Counselor educators are committed to recruiting and retaining a diverse faculty.

F.11.b. Student Diversity

Counselor educators actively attempt to recruit and retain a diverse student body. Counselor educators demonstrate commitment to multicultural/diversity competence by recognizing and valuing diverse cultures and types of abilities students bring to the training experience. Counselor educators provide appropriate accommodations that enhance and support diverse student well-being and academic performance.

F.11.c. Multicultural/Diversity Competence

Counselor educators actively infuse multicultural/diversity competency in their training and supervision practices. They actively train students to gain awareness, knowledge, and skills in the competencies of multicultural practice. Counselor educators include case examples, role-plays, discussion questions, and other classroom activities that promote and represent various cultural perspectives.

Essential Elements

Counselors are committed to promoting and respecting diversity in all phases of the educational process. Counselors work to recruit and retain faculty and students from diverse backgrounds and with diverse cultural identities. For instance, counselor educators give attention to selecting and retaining both students and faculty from different racial, ethnic, religious, gender, and sexual orientation groups. Counselor educators also make an effort to deliberately infuse multicultural competence into all aspects of training. Counselor educators establish and maintain multicultural competence themselves and serve as role models to students and to other faculty in this regard. Counselor educators actively promote the development of multicultural competence by incorporating cross-cultural knowledge and experiences into all aspects of the education process. Additionally, educators make needed accommodations so that students of diverse backgrounds may participate fully in the education and training experience.

Common Dilemmas and Conflicts

- Faculty with Eurocentric or parochial views of the counseling profession and the public we serve are at risk of overlooking the ethical imperative of encouraging multicultural competence.
- Counselors with a narrow view of diversity (e.g., racial only) may overlook students' needs for inclusion; this may diminish the value of the learning environment for culturally different students.
- Faculty who assume that students will learn needed skills in the "diversity course" will miss valuable opportunities to sensitize and train students in multicultural competence.

Prevention and Positive Practice

✓ Take responsibility personally for establishing a welcoming educational environment for students and faculty of all backgrounds and cultural experiences.

✓ Actively inquire of students and other faculty about any accommodations they may need to fully participate in the educational process and then work to implement needed accommodations.

✓ Pursue your own multicultural competence and actively work to expand and maintain it over time.

✓ Integrate sensitivity to and understanding of diversity issues into all of your courses and training activities with students.

✓ When hiring faculty members or recruiting students, work to make the training environment diverse and inclusive; seek students and faculty who represent the full spectrum of diversity.

Section G

Research and Publication

Introduction

Counselors who conduct research are encouraged to contribute to the knowledge base of the profession and promote a clearer understanding of the conditions that lead to a healthy and more just society. Counselors support efforts of researchers by participating fully and willingly whenever possible. Counselors minimize bias and respect diversity in designing and implementing research programs.

Essential Elements

Counselors are encouraged to support behavioral and social science research that is likely to make a contribution to individuals and to society at large. Through willing participation or through the development and implementation of their own research efforts, counselors try to contribute to the knowledge base of the counseling profession. When counselors design or conduct research, they are intentionally attuned to the best interests of individuals and society. Counselors also strive to respect cultural diversity and minimize bias in their research endeavors.

G.1. Research Responsibilities

G.1.a. Use of Human Research Participants

Counselors plan, design, conduct, and report research in a manner that is consistent with pertinent ethical principles, federal and state laws, host institutional regulations, and scientific standards governing research with human research participants.

G.1.b. Deviation From Standard Practice

Counselors seek consultation and observe stringent safeguards to protect the rights of research participants when a research problem suggests a deviation from standard or acceptable practices.

G.1.c. Independent Researchers

When independent researchers do not have access to an Institutional Review Board (IRB), they should consult with researchers who are familiar with IRB procedures to provide appropriate safeguards.

G.1.d. Precautions to Avoid Injury

Counselors who conduct research with human participants are responsible for the welfare of participants throughout the research process and should take reasonable precautions to avoid causing injurious psychological, emotional, physical, or social effects to participants.

G.1.e. Principal Researcher Responsibility

The ultimate responsibility for ethical research practice lies with the principal researcher. All others involved in the research activities share ethical obligations and responsibility for their own actions.

G.1.f. Minimal Interference

Counselors take reasonable precautions to avoid causing disruptions in the lives of research participants that could be caused by their involvement in research.

G.1.g. Multicultural/Diversity Considerations in Research

When appropriate to research goals, counselors are sensitive to incorporating research procedures that take into account cultural considerations. They seek consultation when appropriate.

Essential Elements

When counselors take part in planning, designing, or conducting research of any type, they remain acutely aware of several overarching professional responsibilities. To start with, counselors are responsible for knowing and operating in compliance with all relevant ethical principles, federal and state laws, institutional policies, and prevailing scientific standards. Of equal importance, counselors place the welfare of research participants above all else and take every reasonable precaution to avoid harm—in any form—to participants. Counselors also avoid unnecessary intrusions or disruptions in the lives of participants. When circumstances necessitate a deviation from standard research practices, counselors ensure that the rights and safety of participants are not compromised. Although the primary researcher holds ultimate responsibility for ensuring ethical research practices, all counselors involved in research are accountable for their actions in this context. When not affiliated with an institution or an appropriate review board, counselors actively seek consultation from researchers familiar with current standards of ethical research practice. Finally, counselors who conduct research remain cognizant of cultural variables that might be relevant to the design and outcomes of research efforts.

Common Dilemmas and Conflicts

- Counselors who design and carry out research projects without careful consideration of relevant ethical standards, laws, and institutional policies are at risk in this area.
- Counselors in independent practice may fail to avail themselves of expert consultation or appropriate Institutional Review Board (IRB) review prior to launching a study.
- Failing to remain vigilant to participant distress or discomfort during a research study—especially when the protocol is modified—creates risk of harm or disruption in the lives of participants.

Prevention and Positive Practice

✓ Never design or help to implement a research study without careful consideration of the *ACA Code of Ethics*, laws governing research in your jurisdiction, relevant institutional policies, and current scientific standards for research in your area.

✓ Always place the welfare of research participants first.

✓ Avoid harm and unnecessary disruptions in the lives of participants whenever possible.

✓ Consider relevant cultural variables when designing studies, selecting instruments, and interpreting results.

✓ Submit your research proposals to an appropriate IRB before launching any study; if an IRB is not available, seek consultation from a professional with expertise in your area of research.

✓ Accept full responsibility for the entire research project—including all research participants—if you are the primary researcher; when you are not the primary researcher, accept responsibility for your activities relevant to the project.

✓ When circumstances dictate a deviation from the research protocol, be certain that the change in protocol does not create additional risk for or compromise the rights of participants.

G.2. Rights of Research Participants *(See A.2., A.7.)*

G.2.a. Informed Consent in Research

Individuals have the right to consent to become research participants. In seeking consent, counselors use language that

1. accurately explains the purpose and procedures to be followed,
2. identifies any procedures that are experimental or relatively untried,
3. describes any attendant discomforts and risks,
4. describes any benefits or changes in individuals or organizations that might be reasonably expected,
5. discloses appropriate alternative procedures that would be advantageous for participants,

6. offers to answer any inquiries concerning the procedures,
7. describes any limitations on confidentiality,
8. describes the format and potential target audiences for the dissemination of research findings, and
9. instructs participants that they are free to withdraw their consent and to discontinue participation in the project at any time without penalty.

G.2.b. Deception

Counselors do not conduct research involving deception unless alternative procedures are not feasible and the prospective value of the research justifies the deception. If such deception has the potential to cause physical or emotional harm to research participants, the research is not conducted, regardless of prospective value. When the methodological requirements of a study necessitate concealment or deception, the investigator explains the reasons for this action as soon as possible during the debriefing.

Essential Elements

As a general rule, counselors do not deceive research participants about any aspect of a research study. This is because alternative procedures that do not involve deception are frequently available and because deception may be considered unfair or distressing to participants. If the unique methodological requirements of a study—such as a study of reactions to a social situation—dictate some measure of concealment or deception, counselors inform participants about the deception and the reasons for it during a debriefing at the end of the participants' participation. Deception is never appropriate if it may cause physical or emotional harm to any participant.

Common Dilemmas and Conflicts

- Researchers who are eager to conduct a study involving deception may fail to consider all of the potential reactions on the part of participants.
- Counselors who fail to seek expert consultation or IRB approval prior to conducting a study involving deception are at considerable risk of unethical practice in this area.

Prevention and Positive Practice

✓ Remember that deception, by its very nature, is contradictory to full informed consent.

✓ Never conceal the purpose of an experiment or deceive participants in any way without first considering all viable alternatives and guaranteeing that the deception will not lead to emotional or physical harm.

✓ Always seek—and document—IRB approval or equivalent expert consultation before conducting any study that employs deception.

G.2.c. Student/Supervisee Participation

Researchers who involve students or supervisees in research make clear to them that the decision regarding whether or not to participate in research activities does not affect one's academic standing or supervisory relationship. Students or supervisees who choose not to participate in educational research are provided with an appropriate alternative to fulfill their academic or clinical requirements.

G.2.d. Client Participation

Counselors conducting research involving clients make clear in the informed consent process that clients are free to choose whether or not to participate in research activities. Counselors take necessary precautions to protect clients from adverse consequences of declining or withdrawing from participation.

Essential Elements

Counselors who engage in research and who simultaneously teach, supervise, or provide counseling services are vigilant to avoid pressuring—overtly or subtly—their students, supervisees, or clients to participate in research studies. Counselors naturally hold power in relationships with students, supervisees, and clients. For this reason they are cautious about mixing their roles as teacher/supervisor/counselor with their role as researcher. When students, supervisees, and clients are invited to participate in research, counselors make it clear that there are no adverse consequences for declining or withdrawing, and they arrange alternative assignments or experiences for students or supervisees who elect not to participate.

Common Dilemmas and Conflicts

- Counselors in academic or training settings may erroneously assume that trainees must participate in research as part of the training experience.
- Counselors who underestimate their own power in a professional relationship may subtly and inadvertently coerce clients and students to serve as research participants.
- Blending roles as researcher, therapist, supervisor, or teacher may create potentially harmful multiple relationships.

Prevention and Positive Practice

✓ Be cautious about including students, supervisees, or clients in your research studies.

✓ Recognize your relative power advantage in any professional relationship and the pressure subordinates, students, and clients can feel to "volunteer" as research participants.

✓ Never require trainees to serve as research participants, and always provide alternatives that do not disadvantage trainees in terms of course credit or evaluations.

✓ Remember that a client's experience as a research participant will affect the way in which he or she experiences the counseling relationship.

G.2.e. Confidentiality of Information

Information obtained about research participants during the course of an investigation is confidential. When the possibility exists that others may obtain access to such information, ethical research practice requires that the possibility, together with the plans for protecting confidentiality, be explained to participants as a part of the procedure for obtaining informed consent.

G.2.f. Persons Not Capable of Giving Informed Consent

When a person is not capable of giving informed consent, counselors provide an appropriate explanation to, obtain agreement for participation from, and obtain the appropriate consent of a legally authorized person.

Essential Elements

As is true for counseling clients *(see A.1.a., A.2.)*, research participants have a right to receive full information about the research procedures and any predictable risks and benefits *before* assenting or declining to participate. Informed consent for research participation requires that participants grasp the fundamental procedures involved, their right to refuse or withdraw from participation, and any information that might reasonably affect their willingness to participate. Counselors who design and conduct research studies must only include those participants who have given consent for participation. Informed consent requires the counselor to clearly explain each of the elements of informed consent listed in Standard G.2.a. Counselors place particular emphasis on ensuring that potential participants are informed about the likely risks and benefits of participation in language that participants can understand. If a potential participant is incapable of giving informed consent, counselors seek appropriate informed consent from a legally authorized person, usually the legal guardian.

Common Dilemmas and Conflicts

- Counselors who are in a hurry to launch a research project may fail to give participants adequate informed consent.
- Counselors may be tempted to gloss over or minimize unpleasant or risky aspects of a research design to ensure an adequate sample size.
- Researchers who are inattentive to participants' comprehension level or capacity to provide informed consent may fail to give appropriate and legal informed consent.

Prevention and Positive Practice

✓ Carefully prepare a written informed consent document that covers all elements of informed consent listed in G.2.a., and ensure that research participants understand each element before including them in the research project.

✓ Consider issues of culture, language, and comprehension when determining whether a potential participant is capable of providing informed consent.

✓ When a potential participant is incapable of giving informed consent for research, do not include the person in the research without clear informed consent from a legal guardian.

✓ Always take time to answer questions raised by participants during the informed consent process.

✓ Provide participants with all information that might reasonably be expected to affect their willingness to participate.

G.2.g. Commitments to Participants

Counselors take reasonable measures to honor all commitments to research participants. *(See A.2.c.)*

G.2.h. Explanations After Data Collection

After data are collected, counselors provide participants with full clarification of the nature of the study to remove any misconceptions participants might have regarding the research. Where scientific or human values justify delaying or withholding information, counselors take reasonable measures to avoid causing harm.

G.2.i. Informing Sponsors

Counselors inform sponsors, institutions, and publication channels regarding research procedures and outcomes. Counselors ensure that appropriate bodies and authorities are given pertinent information and acknowledgment.

G.2.j. Disposal of Research Documents and Records

Within a reasonable period of time following the completion of a research project or study, counselors take steps to destroy records or documents (audio, video, digital, and written) containing confidential data or information that identifies research participants. When records are of an artistic nature, researchers obtain participant consent with regard to handling of such records or documents. *(See B.6.g.)*

Essential Elements

Counselors honor their commitments to research participants and those who sponsor, support, and publish their research findings. When engaging in research, counselors are particularly vigilant to protect participant confidentiality *(see B.1.)* and to inform participants in advance of any foreseeable compromise to their confidentiality. Following completion of any research study, counselors dispose of records in a timely fashion and ensure that all records and documents containing confidential information are destroyed *(see B.6.g.)*. When research yields artistic or other potentially meaningful data, counselors secure informed consent from participants regarding disposal of such products. Following completion of a research project, counselors also provide a careful debriefing to participants and take the time to answer participant questions such that they have a clear understanding of the purpose of the research.

Common Dilemmas and Conflicts

- Forgetting that research data must be protected as confidential with the same rigor as client data may increase the risk of confidentiality violations.
- Counselors who are too eager to analyze and disseminate research findings may neglect the crucial steps of debriefing participants and disposing of confidential records of research.

- Counselors who fail to apprise research sponsors and publication outlets of their precise procedures and outcomes may contribute to misinformation about a study.

Prevention and Positive Practice

✓ Be very careful to honor all promises and commitments to research participants.

✓ Protect research participant confidentiality with the same rigor that you protect client confidentiality.

✓ Explain all reasonably predictable compromises to participant confidentiality in advance and work to minimize these to the extent possible.

✓ Properly dispose of research records in accordance with relevant ethical principles, laws, and scientific standards; remember that some institutions, funding sources, and publication outlets specify a minimum amount of time that raw data must be maintained before disposal.

✓ When artistic work is an outcome of a research study, only dispose of such work after obtaining clear informed consent from the research participant.

✓ Immediately following collection of data from a participant, provide a thorough debriefing that includes an explanation of the study's purpose in language the participant can understand.

G.3. Relationships With Research Participants (When Research Involves Intensive or Extended Interactions)

G.3.a. Nonprofessional Relationships

Nonprofessional relationships with research participants should be avoided.

G.3.b. Relationships With Research Participants

Sexual or romantic counselor–research participant interactions or relationships with current research participants are prohibited.

G.3.c. Sexual Harassment and Research Participants

Researchers do not condone or subject research participants to sexual harassment.

G.3.d. Potentially Beneficial Interactions

When a nonprofessional interaction between the researcher and the research participant may be potentially beneficial, the researcher must document, prior to the interaction (when feasible), the rationale for such an interaction, the potential benefit, and anticipated consequences for the research participant. Such interactions should be initiated with the appropriate consent of the research participant. Where unintentional harm occurs to the research participant due to the nonprofessional interaction, the researcher must show evidence of an attempt to remedy such harm.

Essential Elements

When counselors enter into researcher–participant relationships with individuals, they are careful to avoid engaging participants in nonprofessional relationships. This may result in potentially harmful or exploitive multiple relationships *(see A.5.)*. It is always unethical to engage a research participant in a romantic or sexual relationship, and counselors are vigilant to avoid even the appearance of sexual harassment through their actions or comments when interacting with participants. At times, a counselor may have a nonprofessional interaction with a participant (e.g., educationally, collegially). To the extent that this is foreseeable or planned, the counselor must obtain the participant's informed consent and ensure that the nonprofessional interaction is likely to benefit or at least not harm the participant. If unintended harm occurs to a research participant as a result of the interaction, every effort must be made to ameliorate such harm.

Common Dilemmas and Conflicts

- Because research settings may be more informal and less structured than professional counseling settings, it may be tempting to overlook the fact that researcher–participant relationships are professional in nature.
- Counselors who ignore the power differential in research relationships and the danger of exploitation may be at risk in this area.

Prevention and Positive Practice

✓ Avoid nonprofessional relationships with research participants.
✓ Exercise the same judgment regarding boundaries and multiple relationships in research settings that you use in counseling settings.
✓ Remember that sexual relationships with research participants are always unethical.
✓ Never make comments or engage in behavior—including the creation of research materials—that could be considered offensive or harassing to participants.
✓ When tempted to engage a research participant in a nonprofessional interaction, consider whether there is clear potential for benefit to the participant and any risks of harm, and document your reasoning for moving ahead with the interaction.
✓ If a research participant appears distressed or harmed by any nonprofessional interaction with you, make a clear effort to remedy the harm.
✓ Seek collegial consultation before entering into any additional relationship with a research participant.

G.4. Reporting Results

G.4.a. Accurate Results

Counselors plan, conduct, and report research accurately. They provide thorough discussions of the limitations of their data and alternative hypotheses. Counselors do not engage in misleading or fraudulent research, distort data, misrepresent data, or deliberately bias their results. They explicitly mention all variables and conditions known to the investigator that may have affected the outcome of a study or the interpretation of data. They describe the extent to which results are applicable for diverse populations.

G.4.b. Obligation to Report Unfavorable Results

Counselors report the results of any research of professional value. Results that reflect unfavorably on institutions, programs, services, prevailing opinions, or vested interests are not withheld.

G.4.c. Reporting Errors

If counselors discover significant errors in their published research, they take reasonable steps to correct such errors in a correction erratum, or through other appropriate publication means.

G.4.d. Identity of Participants

Counselors who supply data, aid in the research of another person, report research results, or make original data available take due care to disguise the identity of respective participants in the absence of specific authorization from the participants to do otherwise. In situations where participants self-identify their involvement in research studies, researchers take active steps to ensure that data are adapted/changed to protect the identity and welfare of all parties and that discussion of results does not cause harm to participants.

G.4.e. Replication Studies

Counselors are obligated to make available sufficient original research data to qualified professionals who may wish to replicate the study.

Essential Elements

In their research activities, counselors show integrity. Integrity demands that counselors be transparent and honest in reporting research findings and that they avoid any effort at fraud or misrepresentation. Counselors clearly describe the limitations of their research and those variables or conditions that may have affected the results. Integrity also requires counselors to report results that are unfavorable or that undermine their theories or research hypotheses. When they discover errors in their published work, counselors actively work to ensure that public corrections are made. When other professionals request research data for the purpose of replication, counselors comply with these requests while simultaneously ensuring that the identity of research participants is protected; masking the identity of participants before releasing any data is essential.

Common Dilemmas and Conflicts

- Counselors who are under pressure to achieve promotion, maintain grant funding, or get an article published may be tempted to distort or even fabricate data.
- Counselors who become anxious or ashamed may suppress unfavorable research results or fail to make corrections when errors become evident.

- Counselors who are highly competitive or insecure may be inclined to not cooperate with colleagues who request their research data so they may replicate the study.

Prevention and Positive Practice

✓ Be clear and transparent about research procedures and outcomes; never modify, fake, or delete data to achieve a specific outcome.
✓ Clearly discuss the limitations of your hypotheses, research design, and results.
✓ Clearly describe the extent to which your results can be applied to specific groups.
✓ Never suppress or refuse to report research results that do not reflect favorably on your theories, your institution, or your professional work.
✓ When you discover an error—your own or another party's—in a publication or other public presentation of your research work, be proactive in pursuing a correction.
✓ Maintain original research data such that other professionals can replicate or reanalyze your research when this is appropriate.
✓ When providing research data to another professional or displaying them in any forum, be careful to disguise participants such that all personal identifying information is removed.

G.5. Publication

G.5.a. Recognizing Contributions

When conducting and reporting research, counselors are familiar with and give recognition to previous work on the topic, observe copyright laws, and give full credit to those to whom credit is due.

G.5.b. Plagiarism

Counselors do not plagiarize; that is, they do not present another person's work as their own work.

G.5.c. Review/Republication of Data or Ideas

Counselors fully acknowledge and make editorial reviewers aware of prior publication of ideas or data where such ideas or data are submitted for review or publication.

G.5.g. Duplicate Submission

Counselors submit manuscripts for consideration to only one journal at a time. Manuscripts that are published in whole or in substantial part in another journal or published work are not submitted for publication without acknowledgment and permission from the previous publication. (Standard G.5.g. was intentionally included here out of order due to its relevance to the above three Standards.)

Essential Elements

Counselors who engage in the publication or presentation of research or other professional material must be careful to give credit where credit is due. Of course, it is never appropriate to present another's work as your own, but it is equally unethical to borrow significantly from others' work without giving credit to the original authors of those ideas, techniques, or research findings. When submitting manuscripts to editors for review, counselors are transparent about any prior publication of the ideas or data contained in the manuscript, and they never submit a manuscript simultaneously to more than one journal. Although the manuscript review process can be time consuming and frustrating, it is unethical to publish the same material—or largely equivalent material—in more than one publication outlet unless the journal editor(s) are aware of and have approved the overlap in content between publications.

Common Dilemmas and Conflicts

- When counselors feel pressure to publish in order to achieve an academic degree or promotion, they may be tempted to take credit for others' work.
- In an effort to increase the volume of one's publications, it may be tempting to republish the same material or submit a manuscript to more than one outlet at a time.
- Counselors who are careless, overworked, or rushed may inadvertently use others' work without providing appropriate citations.

Prevention and Positive Practice

✓ Whenever you engage in writing for the purpose of publication, be exacting when it comes to tracking the sources of the ideas and fully crediting them with clear and accurate referencing.

✓ Whether using a previous author's ideas, research findings, techniques, or other intellectual material, clearly credit him or her in your own work.

✓ Never submit a journal manuscript to more than one journal at a time; either wait until a manuscript has been rejected by a journal or officially withdraw the manuscript from consideration before resubmitting to another journal.

✓ Remember that publishing substantially the same ideas or research data in more than one manuscript is inappropriate unless the journal editors involved are fully aware of the duplication and the overlap is clearly referenced in the manuscript.

✓ Piecemeal or fragmented publication of data from a single study in several publications may be unethical; always clarify this in advance with journal editors.

G.5.d. Contributors

Counselors give credit through joint authorship, acknowledgment, footnote statements, or other appropriate means to those who have contributed significantly to research or concept development in accordance with such contributions. The principal contributor is listed first, and minor technical or professional contributions are acknowledged in notes or introductory statements.

G.5.e. Agreement of Contributors

Counselors who conduct joint research with colleagues or students/supervisees establish agreements in advance regarding allocation of tasks, publication credit, and types of acknowledgment that will be received.

G.5.f. Student Research

For articles that are substantially based on students' course papers, projects, dissertations or theses, and on which students have been the primary contributors, they are listed as principal authors.

Essential Elements

Counselors recognize that authorship credit is a potentially divisive issue. To be fair and to avoid unnecessary conflict surrounding publication authorship, counselors are deliberate about reaching authorship credit agreements with colleagues and students/supervisees in advance of any research project or manuscript development. Despite such agreements, counselors should remain flexible and willing to reconsider order of authorship and authorship credit should the ultimate contributions of authors change over the course of the project. Order of authorship should be based on relative contribution. Only substantial contributions merit authorship, while minor contributions should be acknowledged with footnotes or a statement of thanks at the outset of a manuscript. As a general rule, any publication based on a student's course project, thesis, or dissertation should list the student as first author.

Common Dilemmas and Conflicts

- Counselors who fail to appreciate the potential for misunderstanding and conflict surrounding authorship may be at risk in this area.
- Those who fail to address authorship issues in advance of a project heighten the risk of conflict with collaborators.
- Counselors who refuse to be flexible and reconsider the relative contributions of those involved at the completion of a project may fail to give appropriate credit to colleagues and students.

Prevention and Positive Practice

✓ Remember that authorship issues have significant professional implications for counselors and other professionals seeking promotion and advancement.

✓ Always discuss authorship issues and seek agreement with all those involved in a research or writing project in advance.

✓ Remain collegial and flexible in revisiting authorship discussions during a project if relative contributions shift and suggest a different order of authorship.

✓ Unless there is a compelling reason not to do so, always list a student or supervisee first when an article or other product is based largely on the student's or supervisee's class project, thesis, or dissertation.

✓ When a colleague or student makes a minor contribution to a project, acknowledge this through an appropriate footnote.

✓ Always seek consultation before making authorship decisions when efforts to resolve conflicts with coauthors informally have not been successful.

G.5.h. Professional Review

Counselors who review material submitted for publication, research, or other scholarly purposes respect the confidentiality and proprietary rights of those who submitted it. Counselors use care to make publication decisions based on valid and defensible standards. Counselors review article submissions in a timely manner and based on their scope and competency in research methodologies. Counselors who serve as reviewers at the request of editors or publishers make every effort to only review materials that are within their scope of competency and use care to avoid personal biases.

Essential Elements

Because scholarly publications have a powerful influence on theory and practice in the field of counseling, counselors who evaluate a colleague's scholarly work as reviewers or editors must approach this responsibility with the utmost care. When counselors review material submitted for publication, they thoroughly protect the author's confidentiality and refrain from discussing or referring to the work in any context. When counselors agree to review and evaluate others' submissions, they are timely, thorough, and fair in their assessments; they work to prevent personal biases—regarding either the author or the topic—from influencing their assessments. Counselors only agree to review manuscript submissions when they believe they have the experience or expertise to render a useful opinion.

Common Dilemmas and Conflicts

- It may be tempting to discuss or refer to a particularly interesting or novel idea or finding after reviewing another author's manuscript.
- Strong personal feelings about an author or counseling theory or technique may lead a reviewer to render an unfair or biased review.
- Counselors with considerable expertise may be inundated with manuscript review requests and may easily fall behind, thereby delaying publication decisions for other professionals.

Prevention and Positive Practice

✓ When you review manuscripts, give them the same confidentiality protections that you accord client notes.

✓ Clearly articulate the boundaries of your competence and experience and do not agree to review manuscripts outside of these boundaries.

✓ If you receive a manuscript for review that is written by a professional with whom you have a personal conflict, close personal or professional relationship, or other conflict of interest, politely refuse to do the review.

✓ If you cannot reasonably complete a manuscript review within the time frame specified by the editor, acknowledge this up front and decline the review.

✓ To the extent possible, avoid allowing your own personal and professional biases to influence your assessment of a manuscript's merits.

Section H

Resolving Ethical Issues

Introduction

Counselors behave in a legal, ethical, and moral manner in the conduct of their professional work. They are aware that client protection and trust in the profession depend on a high level of professional conduct. They hold other counselors to the same standards and are willing to take appropriate action to ensure that these standards are upheld.

Counselors strive to resolve ethical dilemmas with direct and open communication among all parties involved and seek consultation with colleagues and supervisors when necessary. Counselors incorporate ethical practice into their daily professional work. They engage in ongoing professional development regarding current topics in ethical and legal issues in counseling.

Essential Elements

All counselors strive to achieve the highest ideals of the *ACA Code of Ethics* in all their professional behaviors. The welfare and trust of those whom counselors serve are of great importance. Counselors engage in ongoing professional development activities to remain current on ethics and legal issues in counseling. Counselors are accountable for their own conduct and monitor their colleagues' conduct as well. When ethical dilemmas arise, counselors attempt to resolve them using direct and open communication with those involved, and counselors are careful to seek consultation from knowledgeable and experienced colleagues.

Common Dilemmas and Conflicts

- Counselors who do not remain current on ethics and legal standards in counseling practice risk violating these standards and harming clients.
- Counselors who overestimate their knowledge and competence may mismanage ethical dilemmas.
- Counselors who overlook unethical or illegal behaviors by colleagues place clients and the public at risk.

Prevention and Positive Practice

✓ Integrate ethical practice into all aspects of your counseling work.
✓ Address apparently unethical or illegal behaviors by colleagues in a thoughtful and proactive manner.
✓ Remain current on developments in ethics and legal issues in counseling.
✓ Use a decision-making process and active consultation with colleagues when faced with ethics dilemmas.

H.1. Standards and the Law

H.1.a. Knowledge

Counselors understand the *ACA Code of Ethics* and other applicable ethics codes from other professional organizations or from certification and licensure bodies of which they are members. Lack of knowledge or misunderstanding of an ethical responsibility is not a defense against a charge of unethical conduct.

H.1.b. Conflicts Between Ethics and Laws

If ethical responsibilities conflict with law, regulations, or other governing legal authority, counselors make known their commitment to the *ACA Code of Ethics* and take steps to resolve the conflict. If the conflict cannot be resolved by such means, counselors may adhere to the requirements of law, regulations, or other governing legal authority.

Essential Elements

Counselors have a professional obligation to educate themselves about all ethics codes relevant to their certification, licensure, and organizational memberships. Counselors are equally accountable to know and abide by laws relevant to their professional practice. Failure to be familiar with relevant ethics codes or laws is never a justification for unethical or illegal acts. When conflicts occur between the *ACA Code of Ethics* and relevant laws or regulations, counselors attempt to resolve the conflict in keeping with the tenets of the *ACA Code of Ethics.* For instance, when a family court orders the release of a counselor's records such that confidential information about multiple clients might be disclosed—a direct violation of the ACA standard on confidentiality—the counselor would make known this conflict and attempt to find an amicable resolution that addresses the court's need for information without violation of any client's confidentiality. When such resolution is not possible, counselors may follow the law or regulation in question.

Common Dilemmas and Conflicts

- Counselors who do not routinely study and ensure current understanding of ethics codes, laws, and regulations relevant to their professional activities are at risk of ethical and legal transgressions, thereby jeopardizing their professional standing.
- Counselors who blindly follow laws and regulations without careful forethought may be at risk of violating the *ACA Code of Ethics.*

Prevention and Positive Practice

✓ Carefully study the *ACA Code of Ethics* and all applicable laws and regulations relevant to your practice setting.

✓ Update your knowledge of ethics codes, laws, and regulations through ongoing professional development activities.

✓ Always attempt to follow the *ACA Code of Ethics*, but you may follow applicable laws and regulations if they conflict with the code and if your efforts to resolve the conflict have been unsuccessful.

✓ Remember that Standard H.1.b. does not require adherence to a law or regulation; at times, counselors may choose not to follow a law in order to uphold a moral or ethical principle.

✓ When ethical responsibilities conflict with legal requirements, always seek consultation before deciding not to abide by an ethical standard or law.

H.2. Suspected Violations

H.2.a. Ethical Behavior Expected

Counselors expect colleagues to adhere to the *ACA Code of Ethics.* When counselors possess knowledge that raises doubts as to whether another counselor is acting in an ethical manner, they take appropriate action. *(See H.2.b., H.2.c.)*

H.2.b. Informal Resolution

When counselors have reason to believe that another counselor is violating or has violated an ethical standard, they attempt first to resolve the issue informally with the other counselor if feasible, provided such action does not violate confidentiality rights that may be involved.

H.2.c. Reporting Ethical Violations

If an apparent violation has substantially harmed or is likely to substantially harm a person or organization and is not appropriate for informal resolution or is not resolved properly, counselors take further action appropriate to the situation. Such action might include referral to state or national committees on professional ethics, voluntary national certification bodies, state licensing boards, or to the appropriate institutional authorities. This standard does not apply when an intervention would violate confidentiality rights or when counselors have been retained to review the work of another counselor whose professional conduct is in question.

H.2.d. Consultation

When uncertain as to whether a particular situation or course of action may be in violation of the *ACA Code of Ethics,* counselors consult with other counselors who are knowledgeable about ethics and the *ACA Code of Ethics,* with colleagues, or with appropriate authorities.

Essential Elements

All counselors work to ensure ethical conduct by themselves and their colleagues. When they suspect unethical behavior on the part of a colleague, counselors first attempt to resolve the matter informally through open discussion with the colleague. If such informal resolution is not possible or not effective and if substantial harm is evident or likely, counselors file a formal ethics complaint with the appropriate oversight body. Such bodies include ethics committees, certification boards, or licensing boards. Counselors refrain from filing formal complaints when doing so would violate a client's confidentiality. When unsure of how to proceed in such situations, consultation with an experienced colleague is always recommended.

Common Dilemmas and Conflicts

- Counselors who are vindictive or who rush to file formal complaints against colleagues may be at risk of violating this standard.
- Counselors who are uncomfortable with confrontation may fail to take appropriate action even when there is evidence that another professional may harm others.
- When counselors fail to avail themselves of expert consultation, they may be more likely to either overlook colleagues' ethical transgressions or overreact to situations that call for informal resolution.

Prevention and Positive Practice

✓ Attempt to address perceived unethical behavior by colleagues through open discussion and informal resolution if possible.

✓ Never ignore evidence of unethical behavior on the part of a colleague; preventing harm to the public and the profession requires you to be proactive.

✓ When efforts at an informal resolution of a colleague's unethical behavior fail, be prepared to file a formal ethics complaint with the appropriate licensing board or ethics committee.

✓ Never file an ethics complaint if doing so would violate the confidentiality rights of a client.

✓ When faced with ethics dilemmas, always consult with experienced colleagues, ethics committees, or legal experts.

H.2.e. Organizational Conflicts

If the demands of an organization with which counselors are affiliated pose a conflict with the *ACA Code of Ethics,* counselors specify the nature of such conflicts and express to their supervisors or other responsible officials their commitment to the *ACA Code of Ethics*. When possible, counselors work toward change within the organization to allow full adherence to the *ACA Code of Ethics*. In doing so, they address any confidentiality issues.

Essential Elements

If organizational demands appear to be in conflict with the *ACA Code of Ethics*, counselors are obligated to bring such conflicts to the attention of supervisors or organizational leaders. Organizational demands do not trump or supersede counselors' obligations to the *Code of Ethics*. In addition, counselors work to resolve conflicts between ethics and organizational demands by promoting change within the organization that reflects the tenets of the *ACA Code of Ethics*.

Common Dilemmas and Conflicts

- Counselors who assume that all employment requirements and organizational demands are appropriate may be at risk of violating the *ACA Code of Ethics*.
- Failing to address conflicts between organizational policies and ethical obligations is itself a violation of the *Code of Ethics*.

Prevention and Positive Practice

✓ Remain vigilant for organizational policies and practices that may require you to engage in behaviors that are incongruent with the *ACA Code of Ethics*.

✓ Bring conflicts between ethics and organizational demands to the attention of supervisors or other organizational leaders.

✓ Remember that an organizational demand may never trump or supersede an ethical standard.

✓ Whenever possible, work to change organizational policies that conflict with the *ACA Code of Ethics*.

✓ If an organization insists that you adhere to its policies in spite of your efforts to educate policymakers and effect organizational change, seeking legal advice or terminating your association with the organization may be appropriate courses of action.

H.2.f. Unwarranted Complaints

Counselors do not initiate, participate in, or encourage the filing of ethics complaints that are made with reckless disregard or willful ignorance of facts that would disprove the allegation.

H.2.g. Unfair Discrimination Against Complainants and Respondents

Counselors do not deny persons employment, advancement, admission to academic or other programs, tenure, or promotion based solely upon their having made or their being the subject of an ethics complaint. This does not preclude taking action based upon the outcome of such proceedings or considering other appropriate information.

Essential Elements

Counselors never file unwarranted complaints against other professionals for any reason and never take adverse action against any person simply because a person has filed an ethics complaint or is the subject of an ethics complaint.

Common Dilemmas and Conflicts

- Using the ethics complaint process as a way to "get even" with others is a misuse of this process and a violation of this standard.
- Counselors who take adverse employment, admission, or advancement action against a colleague or other person merely on the basis of an ethics complaint may be acting both unethically and illegally.

Prevention and Positive Practice

✓ Before filing—or participating in the filing of—an ethics complaint, be certain that all available evidence points to unethical behavior.

✓ Honestly consider whether a jury of your peers would conclude that your ethics complaint was frivolous or based more on personal dislike than genuine evidence.

✓ Never take action against colleagues, students, or others simply because they have filed an ethics complaint or are the subject of an ethics complaint.

H.3. Cooperation With Ethics Committees

> Counselors assist in the process of enforcing the *ACA Code of Ethics.* Counselors cooperate with investigations, proceedings, and requirements of the ACA Ethics Committee or ethics committees of other duly constituted associations or boards having jurisdiction over those charged with a violation. Counselors are familiar with the *ACA Policies and Procedures for Processing Complaints of Ethical Violations* and use it as a reference for assisting in the enforcement of the *ACA Code of Ethics.*

Essential Elements

If an ethics complaint is ever filed against a counselor, full cooperation with the investigation and related proceedings is required under the *ACA Code of Ethics.* Similar cooperation is required of counselors when investigations and proceedings are initiated by licensure or certification boards. Further, counselors cooperate in ethics investigations focusing on other professionals. Finally, counselors must be familiar with the *ACA Policies and Procedures for Processing Complaints of Ethical Violations* and utilize this document to assist in the enforcement of the *ACA Code of Ethics.*

Common Dilemmas and Conflicts

- Counselors who want to avoid sanctions for unethical behaviors may be tempted not to cooperate with ethics committee or licensing board investigation processes or proceedings.
- Counselors who are not familiar with the *ACA Policies and Procedures for Processing Complaints of Ethical Violations* place themselves at risk when facing an investigation or proceedings.

Prevention and Positive Practice

✓ Cooperate fully with all ethics investigations and proceedings.
✓ Never alter or destroy records, or coerce other individuals, in an attempt to avoid sanctions.
✓ Recognize that failure to cooperate with ethics investigations is itself an ethics infraction.
✓ Be knowledgeable of all rules, policies, regulations, and laws relevant to the conduct of investigations, hearings, and other proceedings.

Glossary of Terms

The following are the definitions of a number of terms used throughout the *ACA Code of Ethics*. Familiarity with them will make understanding and applying the *ACA Code of Ethics* an easier task for counselors, thus helping counselors to more closely follow its dictates and to practice counseling ethically.

Advocacy: promotion of the well-being of individuals, groups, and the counseling profession within systems and organizations. Advocacy seeks to remove barriers and obstacles that inhibit access, growth, and development.

Assent: to demonstrate agreement, when a person is otherwise not capable or competent to give formal consent (e.g., informed consent) to a counseling service or plan.

Client: an individual seeking or referred to the professional services of a counselor for help with problem resolution or decision making.

Counselor: a professional (or a student who is a counselor-in-training) engaged in a counseling practice or other counseling-related services. Counselors fulfill many roles and responsibilities, such as counselor educators, researchers, supervisors, practitioners, and consultants.

Counselor Educator: a professional counselor engaged primarily in developing, implementing, and supervising the educational preparation of counselors-in-training.

Counselor Supervisor: a professional counselor who engages in a formal relationship with a practicing counselor or counselor-in-training for the purpose of overseeing that individual's counseling work or clinical skill development.

Culture: membership in a socially constructed way of living that incorporates collective values, beliefs, norms, boundaries, and lifestyles that are cocreated with others who share similar worldviews comprising biological, psychosocial, historical, psychological, and other factors.

Diversity: the similarities and differences that occur within and across cultures, and the intersection of cultural and social identities.

Documents: any written, digital, audio, visual, or artistic recording of the work within the counseling relationship between counselor and client.

Examinee: a recipient of any professional counseling service that includes educational, psychological, and career appraisal utilizing qualitative or quantitative techniques.

Forensic Evaluation: any formal assessment conducted for court or other legal proceedings.

Multicultural/Diversity Competence: a capacity whereby counselors possess cultural and diversity awareness and knowledge about self and others, and how this awareness and knowledge is applied effectively in practice with clients and client groups.

Multicultural/Diversity Counseling: counseling that recognizes diversity and embraces approaches that support the worth, dignity, potential, and uniqueness of individuals within their historical, cultural, economic, political, and psychosocial contexts.

Student: an individual engaged in formal educational preparation as a counselor-in-training.

Supervisee: a professional counselor or counselor-in-training whose counseling work or clinical skill development is being overseen in a formal supervisory relationship by a qualified trained professional.

Supervisor: counselors who are trained to oversee the professional clinical work of counselors and counselors-in-training.

Teaching: all activities engaged in as part of a formal educational program designed to lead to a graduate degree in counseling.

Training: the instruction and practice of skills related to the counseling profession. Training contributes to the ongoing proficiency of students and professional counselors.

PART II

Decision Making and Ethical Practice in Counseling

An Ethical Decision-Making Process for Counselors

Introduction

Counselors are regularly faced with a wide range of dilemmas and situations that are both ethically and clinically challenging. The *ACA Code of Ethics* is an essential resource for addressing these challenges and dilemmas. In fact, failure to be aware of and to consult the *ACA Code of Ethics* in these situations would itself constitute an ethical problem. As Standard H.1.a. so clearly states, "Lack of knowledge or misunderstanding of an ethical responsibility is not a defense against a charge of unethical conduct." Thus, a detailed knowledge of the *ACA Code of Ethics* is essential for all counselors. Part I of *Ethics Desk Reference for Counselors* is designed to assist counselors in their efforts to effectively use and apply the *ACA Code of Ethics* when faced with these situations. Part I also outlines key steps to take to prevent many of the more commonly faced dilemmas and challenging situations.

However, even the most thoughtful counselor will face challenges that cannot be prevented or avoided. Further, dilemmas will arise that are not specifically addressed in the *ACA Code of Ethics.* While the *ACA Code of Ethics* provides valuable guidance across a broad range of counseling situations and settings, it is not designed to anticipate and address every dilemma or ethically challenging situation. To augment the use of the *ACA Code of Ethics,* one needs thoughtful application of a model for ethical decision making. This is provided in Part II. The use of this model should be of great value to counselors in their efforts to reason through both mundane ethical questions and the more prickly quagmires that offer no apparent right answer or clear course of action. By applying the nine stages of this model, counselors will have a step-by-step process for working through ethical dilemmas and determining the most reasonable actions.

In addition, several areas of counseling practice pose consistent challenges for counselors—regardless of their level of preparation or experience. For instance, remembering the ethical issues in play and the best steps to take when a client is suicidal or when you become the subject of an ethics complaint is challenging indeed. In Part II of this guide, we have therefore identified several specific counseling situations or contexts most likely to provoke ethical questions and conflicts. These areas include ethical issues regarding culture and diversity, confidentiality, exceptions to confidentiality, boundaries and multiple relationships in counseling, competence, counseling suicidal clients, supervision, managed care, termination and abandonment, and responding to subpoenas and court orders, lawsuits, and ethics complaints. Each of these special areas of ethical concern is tackled in Part II. Each of the chapters in Part II offers helpful information to guide counselors in that area of counseling practice. These chapters are provided to assist counselors to both prevent dilemmas and respond to them thoughtfully when they arise. Topics in Part II are considered essential to ethical and competent counseling practice; each covers a domain most often fraught with ethical dilemmas and challenges. Finally, those seeking additional guidance on ethical decision making in the field of counseling should consult the list of resources provided in the Appendix.

Making good ethical decisions can be difficult for even the most experienced counselors. Ethical concerns and conflicts may strike suddenly, and counseling professionals can easily feel blindsided, upset, or overwhelmed on these occasions. Because counselors are human and because human emotional reactions to conflicts or ethics complaints may include dysfunctional responses such as denial, panic, or impulsive anger, it is imperative that counselors develop a clear approach to facing ethical dilemmas.

Although the *ACA Code of Ethics* is an essential tool for making good decisions, remember that finding the right solution to an ethical problem will require more than mere knowledge of the *Code of Ethics*. No ethics code can possibly address every situation or dilemma a counselor may face, and at times, ethical standards alone may not fully address a client's best interests. Further, there will be occasions in which an ethical standard may appear to conflict with a law or times when competing ethical standards appear to suggest different courses of action (Rowley & MacDonald, 2001).

Making sound ethical decisions requires counselors to slow down the decision-making process and to engage in a coherent and intentional course of ethical deliberation, consultation, and action. Wise counselors resist the urge to react instantly to complaints or dilemmas and instead invoke a clear process of exploring facts, reviewing relevant principles and standards, and considering the best interests of those they serve. Good decision making requires counselors to resist a rigid or oversimplified application of the *Code of Ethics*.

The Nine Stages of Ethical Decision Making

Below, we offer a model for making good ethical decisions. Think of this as a tried-and-true process for arriving at the best decision possible. Based on the best elements of several existing decision-making models, this is a process we recommend for all mental health professionals (Barnett & Johnson, 2008; Cottone & Claus, 2000; Forester-Miller & Davis, 1996; Kitchener, 1984). Think of this as a strategy to use when you are confronted with an ethical concern, quandary, or even a complaint. Keep in mind that many ethical dilemmas have no readily apparent, clearly right or wrong answer. The goal of a decision-making process is to assist you to consider all relevant facts, use all available resources, and reason through the dilemma, arriving at the best possible course of action based on available evidence (Kitchener, 2000). Further, this is a dynamic process, and as available information, resources, and circumstances change, your course of action may change as well.

Stage 1: Define the Situation Clearly

- ✓ Articulate the nature of the situation.
- ✓ Gather as many relevant facts and details as possible.
- ✓ Pinpoint the primary quandary or conflict(s).
- ✓ Begin to consider the potential ethical issues and your obligations.

Stage 2: Determine Who Will Be Affected

- ✓ Identify the primary clients as well as any secondary clients.
- ✓ Consider the full range of persons who might be affected by your decision.
- ✓ Articulate your professional obligations to and the rights of each person and group involved.
- ✓ Be especially sensitive to the potential for harm to any person involved.
- ✓ Reflect on your obligation to promote the best interests of those involved.
- ✓ Begin to consider the potential impact of various decisions on those involved.

Stage 3: Refer to Both Underlying Ethical Principles (Beauchamp & Childress, 2001; Kitchener, 1984) and the Standards of the *ACA Code of Ethics*

- ✓ Ask yourself the following principle-based questions:
    1. How can I contribute to my client's welfare (beneficence)?
    2. How can I avoid harming my client and others (nonmaleficence)?
    3. How can I promote my client's independence (autonomy)?
    4. How can I remain loyal to my client (fidelity)?
    5. How can I ensure equitable treatment of clients (fairness)?
    6. How can I protect my client's disclosures (privacy)?
- ✓ Review the *ACA Code of Ethics.*
- ✓ Identify the standards and universal principles most germane to your situation.
- ✓ When specific standards are ambiguous regarding your question, consider the more fundamental obligations conveyed in the universal ethical principles.
- ✓ Consider consulting one or more current ethics texts or articles on ethics in professional journals for additional guidance or case examples.

Stage 4: Refer to Relevant Laws/Regulations and Professional Guidelines

- ✓ Review legal statutes and regulations bearing on counseling in your jurisdiction.
- ✓ Consider agency and institutional policies.
- ✓ Identify and review any relevant counseling guidelines bearing on the situation, client type, problem, and type of service.
- ✓ Consult with a lawyer to determine your legal obligations and the legal consequences of various courses of action.
- ✓ Consult with colleagues or ethics organizations concerning potential conflicts between ethical and legal obligations.

Stage 5: Reflect Honestly on Personal Feelings and Competence

- ✓ Take time to reflect honestly about the thoughts and feelings aroused by the situation.
- ✓ Consider whether feelings aroused about yourself (e.g., shame, diminished esteem) or others involved (e.g., anger, anxiety, sexual attraction) may negatively affect your decision making.
- ✓ Honestly consider whether you have the requisite competence—defined by education, training, and supervised experience—to handle the situation effectively.

Stage 6: Consult With Trusted Colleagues

- ✓ Carefully select one or more colleagues whom you know to have experience, good judgment, solid familiarity with ethical and legal issues, and, preferably, experience in the area of concern.
- ✓ Seek consultant referrals, if needed, from local or national counseling organizations.
- ✓ Select consultants who are honest, forthright, and respectful of confidentiality.
- ✓ Prepare carefully for the consultation by summarizing key facts, apparent ethical issues, personal concerns, and possible courses of action.

Stage 7: Formulate Alternative Courses of Action

- ✓ Take time to think about the full range of possible responses to the situation.
- ✓ Consider all of the ways you might proceed in light of the facts at hand (e.g., full array of interventions, research designs, methods of confronting a student or colleague).
- ✓ Consider the feasibility and ethical/legal implications of each approach.

Stage 8: Consider Possible Outcomes for All Parties Involved

- ✓ Evaluate the probable impact—for each client and stakeholder—of each course of action considered.
- ✓ Enumerate possible outcomes for those involved, paying particular attention to potential risks and benefits.
- ✓ Assess the implications of each approach in light of your ethical and legal obligations.
- ✓ Document this reasoning process.

Stage 9: Make a Decision and Monitor the Outcome

- ✓ Based on the first eight stages and all relevant information available to you at this time, select the best option and implement it.
- ✓ When possible, discuss your decision and your rationale with stakeholders.
- ✓ Always take full responsibility for the decision.
- ✓ Carefully monitor—to the extent possible—the effects of your course of action on those involved. Modify your plan as needed and continue this process until the best possible outcomes are achieved.
- ✓ Clearly document each stage of your ethical decision-making process.

References

Barnett, J. E., & Johnson, W. B. (2008). *Ethics desk reference for psychologists.* Washington, DC: American Psychological Association.

Beauchamp, T. L., & Childress, J. F. (2001). *Principles of biomedical ethics* (5th ed.). New York: Oxford University Press.

Cottone, R. R., & Claus, R. E. (2000). Ethical decision making models: A review of the literature. *Journal of Counseling & Development, 78,* 275–283.

Forester-Miller, H., & Davis, T. (1996). *A practitioner's guide to ethical decision making.* Retrieved from http://www.counseling.org/resources/pracguide.htm

Kitchener, K. S. (1984). Intuition, critical evaluation, and ethical principles: The foundation for ethical decisions in counseling psychology. *Counseling Psychologist, 12,* 43–55.

Kitchener, K. S. (2000). *Foundations of ethical practice, research and teaching in psychology.* Mahwah, NJ: Erlbaum.

Rowley, W. J., & MacDonald, D. (2001). Counseling and the law: A cross-cultural perspective. *Journal of Counseling & Development, 79,* 422–429.

Ethical Issues Regarding Culture and Diversity

The *ACA Code of Ethics* emphasizes that counselors are ethically obligated to work at understanding the diverse cultural backgrounds of the clients they serve *(see Standard C.2.a.)*. Changing demographics make it imperative for counselors to respect client diversity in all its forms and to explore their own cultural identities and how these affect their values and beliefs about the counseling process. To the extent that counselors remain culturally encapsulated, that is, focused on the values of the dominant culture and insensitive to variations among groups and individuals, they are at risk for practicing unethically *(see Standard C.5.)* (Arrendondo et al., 1996). The *ACA Code of Ethics* recognizes the real danger of inflicting harm when counselors fail to recognize, appreciate, and effectively address cultural dynamics in their counseling work.

Increasingly, the counseling practice will be multicultural or defined by working to help individuals or groups from different cultural backgrounds and with differing worldviews. The culturally pluralistic or responsive counselor recognizes the complexity of culture, values, and diversity. These counselors embrace a multicultural approach and demonstrate a commitment to developing the knowledge, skills, and self-awareness necessary to work effectively with diverse clients. Not only do they endeavor to understand the diverse backgrounds and social identities of their clients, they are equally invested in becoming aware of their personal cultural heritage and exploring how their own cultural identities influence their values, beliefs, biases, and reactions to persons from different cultures *(see Standard A.4.b.)*. Finally, ethical counseling across culture requires the counselor to promote respect for human dignity across the full spectrum of human diversity (e.g., age, race, ethnicity, gender, gender identity, sexual orientation, religion/spirituality, disability, and socioeconomic status) *(see Standard A.1.a.)*.

Ethical decision making in a multicultural context begins with adequate personal and professional preparation to work with diverse groups. It requires a genuine commitment to becoming competent with specific cultural groups and a sincere respect for the beliefs, attitudes, practices, and worldviews of different clients. Of course, effective multicultural counseling requires knowledge of the many standards of the *ACA Code of Ethics* bearing on diversity and the ability to balance ethical standards with the realities of the cultural experience of individual clients (Sue & Sue, 2003).

Here are several recommendations for ethical multicultural counseling. Each recommendation originates in one of the standards from the *ACA Code of Ethics*. Consider each recommendation carefully when you provide any service to a culturally different client.

Actively Seek Cultural Competence

Counselors practice only within the boundaries of their competence based on appropriate education, training, supervised experience, credentials, and appropriate professional experience *(see Standard C.2.)*. The *ACA Code of Ethics* emphasizes that you should avoid counseling members of diverse client groups if you are unfamiliar with these groups and lack appropriate knowledge, sensitivities, and skills relevant to these groups *(see Standard C.2.a.)*. Although it is not realistic to develop expertise with every culture or subculture, you should take active steps to increase competence with those groups you plan to serve. If you know you will be working with a client with a salient cultural identity distinct from your own (e.g., race, sexual orientation, disability), consider the following methods for achieving the requisite competence:

- Meet with a supervisor or consultant with expert knowledge about the culture. Engage in discussion and supervision designed to enhance your knowledge, sensitivity, and counseling skill relevant to the culture in question.
- Engage in reading, course work, or continuing education relevant to the cultural group and related counseling issues.
- Familiarize yourself with guidelines such as ACA's Multicultural Counseling Competencies and Standards and Cross-Cultural Competencies and Objectives (http://www.counseling.org/Resources/).

Pursue Awareness of Your Own Cultural Values and Biases

You are responsible for becoming aware of your own personal needs, values, and worldview before attempting to work with others. Becoming culturally self-aware necessitates an appreciation of your own cultural heritage, including assumptions and biases regarding other groups. More important, you must avoid imposing personal values and respect the diversity of clients, trainees, and research participants *(see Standard A.4.b.)*.

Do Not Condone or Engage in Discrimination

The *ACA Code of Ethics* is clear: You must never discriminate against clients, trainees, or research participants based on any diversity variable such as age, culture, disability, ethnicity, race, religion/spirituality, gender, gender identity, sexual orientation, marital status/partnership, language preference, or socioeconomic status *(see Standard C.5.)*. You must additionally prevent those you supervise from engaging in such discrimination. Never ignore evidence of discrimination such that your behavior may communicate tacit approval.

Understand and Respect Clients' Attitudes and Values Regarding Counseling

Many of your clients may hold views about appropriate counseling relationship behavior that differ markedly from your own. For instance, some clients may view self-disclosure, interpersonal warmth, or assertiveness as inappropriate to a professional relationship with an authority figure. Members of certain cultural groups may have attitudes and practices in relation to giving gifts, physical contact, and personal space that vary markedly from traditional Western norms. As a counselor, it is your job to maintain awareness and sensitivity regarding the cultural meanings of specific counseling expectations and counselor behavior *(see Standard B.1.a.)* (Constantine & Sue, 2005).

Take Time With Informed Consent

When working across cultures, take time to communicate information in ways that are culturally appropriate. For instance, when a client has difficulty understanding the language you speak, you should provide necessary services such as a qualified interpreter *(see Standard A.2.c.)*. When providing informed consent, take time to ensure that clients grasp the parameters of confidentiality, and respect the fact that clients may have culturally distinct views about the disclosure of confidential information.

Be Especially Careful to Provide Informed Consent for Assessment

Prior to conducting an assessment on a client from a different culture, take adequate time to explain the purposes of assessment and how the results may be used *(see Standard E.3.a.)*. Be sure to provide this explanation in a language the client can understand while remaining sensitive to the client's cultural understanding of testing and assessment (Fisher & Chambers, 2003).

Use Caution When Selecting Assessment Instruments and Techniques

As a counselor, you must be particularly cautious when selecting assessment techniques. Always ensure that tests were normed on the client's population and that the instrument's psychometric properties with that group are established. Also, be sure that you have the competence to recognize the effects of the client's culture on test administration and interpretation *(see Standards E.6.c., E.8.)*. Cultural competence in assessment requires that you can accurately place the client's assessment results in proper perspective given the client's primary cultural group(s) and other relevant factors (Dana, 1996).

Think Twice Before Rendering a Diagnosis

Multicultural competence requires that you develop an appreciation of the problems of discrimination, oppression, and racism in society, and, more importantly, in the mental health care disciplines. Be sure to recognize the historical and social prejudices at work in the misdiagnosis and pathologizing of certain cultural groups *(see Standard E.5.c.)*. Avoid attributing reluctance to cooperate with assessment as a sign of pathology, and recognize that your cultural and training experiences affect the way that you define client problems. Carefully consider the ways in which clients' socioeconomic and cultural experiences may influence behavior, including symptom presentation, before rendering any diagnosis *(see Standard E.5.b.)* (Kleinman, 1993).

Support Clients' Cultural Networks

Recognize that support networks can hold a wide range of meanings in the lives of clients and that these networks may have profound significance for different cultural groups. Work collaboratively with clients to better understand the meaning of cultural networks and, with your client's consent, consider the value of involving network members such as religious/spiritual/community leaders, family members, and friends in the counseling process *(see Standard A.1.d.)*.

Demonstrate Flexibility With Respect to Bartering and Receiving Gifts

Recognize that in some cultures, small gifts are a token of respect and showing gratitude. It is often culturally sensitive and appropriate to accept such small gifts as a means of acknowledging the client's gratitude as long as the gift is not so valuable as to constitute exploitation *(see Standard A.10.e.)* (Brown & Trangsrud, 2008). Similarly, some clients—particularly those from lower socioeconomic groups—may rely on bartering to secure needed counseling services. It is important to consider the cultural implications of bartering and to discuss any concerns you have with clients at the outset *(see Standard A.10.d.)*.

Make Appropriate Referrals When You Lack Cultural Competence

As in other areas of your counseling practice, know when to make referrals to competent colleagues when you lack the competencies to work with a culturally different client. In this situation the *ACA Code of Ethics* requires counselors to be knowledgeable about culturally and clinically appropriate referral sources and to suggest these as alternatives to clients when relevant *(see Standard A.11.d.)*.

Be Alert to the Role of Diversity in the Supervisory Relationship

In your supervisory relationships, be aware of and respectfully address the role of cultural and diversity issues *(see Standard F.2.b.)*. It is important to be both sensitive to diversity differences and willing to openly discuss them in the supervisory relationship.

Infuse Counselor Training Programs With Multiculturalism

As a counselor educator, you are responsible for ensuring that multiculturalism and diversity are prominent features of the training programs with which you affiliate *(see Standards F.6., F.11.)* (Fisher & Chambers, 2003). Here are several ways that you can achieve this objective:

- When preparing a counseling class or workshop curriculum, think of ways to infuse the syllabus, lectures, and assignments with material and experiences related to diversity and culture.
- When recruiting faculty for your program, give particular attention to methods for attracting and retaining diverse faculty members.
- Find innovative methods for recruiting and retaining a diverse student body; when selecting students, find ways to recognize and value the diverse cultures and types of abilities students may bring to the program.
- When training and supervising, actively infuse the development of multiculturalism and diversity competence; deliberately foster cross-cultural knowledge, attitudes, self-awareness, and counseling skills when teaching and supervising trainees (Hays, 2008).
- In your teaching and training, find creative ways to impart multicultural knowledge and competencies to students and trainees (e.g., case examples, role-plays, discussion questions, and activities that foster awareness and respect of different cultures).

Design and Implement Culturally Appropriate Research Studies

When conceptualizing and conducting research, be careful to incorporate procedures that take into account participant culture *(see Standard G.1.g.)* (Gil & Bob, 1999). Always work to minimize bias and respect diversity when designing research. Ensure that participants in research are representative of the general population. When planning research, consider the value of studying issues relevant to all groups, not just the majority population (Peña, 2007).

References

Arrendondo, P., Toporek, R., Brown, S. P., Jones, J., Locke, D., Sanchez, J., & Stadler, H. (1996). Operationalization of the multicultural counseling competencies. *Journal of Multicultural Counseling and Development, 24,* 42–78.

Brown, C., & Trangsrud, H. B. (2008). Factors associated with acceptance and decline of client gift giving. *Professional Psychology: Research and Practice, 39,* 505–511.

Constantine, M. G., & Sue, D. W. (Eds.). (2005). *Strategies for building multicultural competence in mental health and educational settings.* New York: Wiley.

Dana, R. H. (1996). Culturally competent assessment practice in the United States. *Journal of Personality Assessment, 66,* 472–487.

Fisher, J. M., & Chambers, E. (2003). Multicultural counseling ethics and assessment competencies: Directions for counselor education programs. *Journal of Applied Rehabilitation Counseling, 34*(2), 17–21.

Gil, E. F., & Bob, S. (1999). Culturally competent research: An ethical perspective. *Clinical Psychological Review, 19,* 45–55.

Hays, D. G. (2008). Assessing multicultural competence in counselor trainees: A review of instrumentation and future directions. *Journal of Counseling & Development, 86,* 95–101.

Kleinman, A. (1993, January). How is culture important for *DSM–IV*? In NIMH-Sponsored Group on Culture and Diagnosis, *Cultural proposals and supporting papers for* DSM-IV (pp. 12–31). Pittsburgh, PA: University of Pittsburgh.

Peña, E. D. (2007). Lost in translation: Methodological considerations in cross-cultural research. *Child Development, 78,* 1255–1264.

Sue, D. W., & Sue, D. (2003). *Counseling the culturally different: Theory and practice* (4th ed.). New York: Wiley.

Confidentiality

Confidentiality is essential for a successful counseling relationship. Clients share their most personal thoughts in an atmosphere of trust in the hope of receiving much-needed assistance. Without the promise of confidentiality, many potential clients would likely not pursue or participate in counseling. The promise of confidentiality enables clients to openly discuss what troubles them *(see Standard B.1.c.)*.

Of course, there are many threats to confidentiality. Counselors must use forethought and vigilance to minimize risks to confidentiality. To reduce the probability of inadvertent disclosures of confidential information, we offer the following recommendations.

Provide Clear Informed Consent

Apprise every client about how confidentiality will be addressed and preserved in the counseling relationship *(see Standard B.1.d.)*. Clients may naturally assume that everything they discuss with you will be held in the strictest confidence. To avoid distress or feelings of betrayal, review any limits to confidentiality that can be reasonably anticipated prior to allowing the client to disclose personal information. For example, if treatment information will or may at any point be shared with parents, employers, or other third parties, let clients know this up front.

Inform Couples, Families, and Groups About the Unique Risks to Confidentiality Generated by These Counseling Contexts

Remember that when more than one client is present for counseling, confidentiality is often more difficult to preserve. Clarify all expectations regarding confidentiality at the outset of the counseling relationship *(see Standards B.4.a., B.4.b.)*. Responsibilities and obligations of clients for others' confidential information should be clearly established at the outset and periodically reviewed over the course of couples, family, or group counseling (Kell, 1999). Further, in these counseling situations with more than one client, counselors make clear from the outset their policies regarding how they will treat communications to them from one party and specify if these communications will be kept confidential or shared with the other client(s) at the next counseling session.

Pay Special Attention to Office Design

Soundproofing

You should thoroughly assess how conversations in your consultation room carry; ensure that those outside the room are not able to overhear counseling sessions (Zur, 2007). For instance, have two people conduct a loud conversation in your office and, with the door closed, see if you can hear them in the hallway, waiting room, or the rooms next door. Also, consider adding soundproofing to the walls, ceiling, and possibly door as needed to ensure confidentiality.

Use of White Noise

There may be limits to the availability or effectiveness of soundproofing efforts; therefore, you should also consider using white noise machines or music in your waiting room or in the hallway right outside your office door to further reduce the risk of having your counseling sessions overheard outside the consultation room.

Office Setup

It is important to ensure that clients and others in your waiting room do not overhear confidential conversations. If a receptionist or secretary is stationed in the waiting area, no telephone conversations with clients should occur where others may overhear them. The use of a sliding glass partition that separates the workstation from the waiting room is a widely used solution.

Clarify Office Practices and Procedures

Never leave client records out where they may be read or even viewed by others. Remember that your clients may easily notice the names on client records inadvertently left out on your desk. Likewise, you should never place client records for filing on the secretary's desk or elsewhere in the waiting room where unauthorized individuals may see them. When multiple counselors share an office and filing system, it is important that they each sign a specific privacy policy statement. No one should access a client's record unless they are treating that client or have received written permission from the client for such access.

Take Responsibility for Staff Training

Be sure to carefully train all of your subordinates, including supervisees, trainees, and staff; you are responsible for ensuring their understanding of confidentiality requirements *(see Standard B.3.a.)*. Periodically brief your staff on the requirements of the *ACA Code of Ethics*; you should additionally monitor their performance in this regard. Avoid assuming that your staff and other subordinates are thoroughly aware of, sensitive to, and vigilant about protecting confidentiality; even the most experienced among us benefit from occasional reminders in this area.

Be Cautious When Responding to Requests for Information

While counselors endeavor to be responsive to valid requests for information, it is essential that you first examine the appropriateness of any request. You may only release records and other information relevant to a client's counseling with appropriate authorization from the client or other responsible party such as a parent or guardian for a minor client *(see Standard B.6.f.)* (Smith-Bell & Winslade, 1994). This authorization should be provided in writing and should specify exactly what may be released and to whom. Further, all authorizations to release information should include a date that specifies when the permission to release information expires. You should never respond to a request for information over the telephone, even if the other party states that it is an emergency situation; always obtain written consent to ensure that you respect and preserve each client's rights.

Monitor Record Storage and Disposal

Store all counseling records securely, such as in a locked file cabinet in a locked room. Never leave records out on your desk, even if only for a few minutes. If records must be taken out of the office, take special care to protect their integrity and prevent any unauthorized person from seeing them *(see Standard B.6.a.)*. When disposing of records, adhere to all applicable laws bearing on the timing and appropriate methods for destroying client records *(see Standard B.6.g.)*. A counseling record that is to be disposed should be shredded—or otherwise destroyed—to ensure that unauthorized access to the record cannot occur in the future. Remember that you are responsible for guaranteeing that records are carefully destroyed (Mitchell, 2007).

Inform Clients About Consultation and Supervision

Although consultation and supervision are important practices that help to ensure that your clients receive the best possible counseling services, you must first secure your clients' consent to such activities before sharing any confidential information with consultants or supervisors. Even when your clients provide written informed consent, make it a practice to share only the minimum identifying information about clients required for the purposes of consultation *(see Standard B.8.c.)*.

Be Thoughtful About Using Technology

Many technologies may help you to practice with greater efficiency and may be of great value to clients who have the need to communicate with you in between counseling sessions. However, the use of technology in counseling practice brings with it a number of ethical risks and, specifically, threats to confidentiality (Shapiro & Schulman, 1996). You should exercise careful forethought to help ensure that client confidentiality is preserved and protected when utilizing these technologies *(see Standard B.3.e.)*.

Computers, E-mail, and the Internet

The use of computers may greatly increase your efficiency, but confidential information stored in a computer places your clients' privacy at risk. All computer access should be password controlled, antivirus software should be used and kept up to date to ensure that confidential information may not be inappropriately accessed, and all information stored on a computer should be backed up on a disk that is stored in a secure location.

The use of e-mail is not confidential, and anyone who can access the server through which the e-mail message is routed may have access to it. E-mail communication with clients should only occur after clients are informed of the risks involved. If e-mail is used to discuss clinical or other confidential information, as may be the case in remote environments or during an extended absence on the part of you or the client, then encryption software should be used to prevent unwanted access to e-mail exchanges *(see also Standards A.12.e., A.12.g.)* (Barnett & Scheetz, 2003).

Telephones and Cell Phones

Always be sure of the identity of the person you are speaking with before releasing confidential information. During the informed consent process, find out where the client prefers to be contacted (home, work, or cell phone). Be sure that clients understand the threats to privacy that may exist when using cell phones. Be careful to only speak with clients in a location where you cannot be overheard by others.

Leaving Messages and Making Calls

When asking for your client or leaving messages, do not mention any confidential information and do not disclose the nature of the call. Do not provide any information that the client would not want others to hear.

Fax Machines

Always use a cover sheet that specifically states the confidential nature of the material included in the fax. Include your telephone number and request that any materials received in error be destroyed or returned to you. Be sure of the location of the receiving fax machine and whether others may have access to faxes that you send on behalf of clients. Always check the number you input into the fax machine for accuracy before pushing the send button.

References

Barnett, J. E., & Scheetz, K. (2003). Technological advances and telehealth: Ethics, law, and the practice of psychology. *Psychotherapy: Theory/Research/Practice/Training, 40,* 86–93.

Kell, C. (1999). Confidentiality and the counselor in general practice. *British Journal of Guidance and Counseling, 27,* 431–440.

Mitchell, R. W. (2007). *Documentation in counseling records: An overview of ethical, legal, and clinical issues* (3rd ed.). Alexandria, VA: American Counseling Association.

Shapiro, D. E., & Schulman, C. E. (1996). Ethical and legal issues in e-mail therapy. *Ethics and Behavior, 6,* 107–124.

Smith-Bell, M., & Winslade, W. J. (1994). Privacy, confidentiality, and privilege in psychotherapeutic relationships. *American Journal of Orthopsychiatry, 64,* 180–193.

Zur, O. (2007). The home office practice. In O. Zur, *Boundaries in psychotherapy: Ethical and clinical explorations* (pp. 119–131). Washington, DC: American Psychological Association.

Exceptions to Confidentiality

Counselors should be familiar with laws in their jurisdiction relevant to the release of confidential information obtained through the counseling relationship. Such laws include mandatory reporting requirements for suspected abuse or neglect of a minor; suspected abuse or neglect of an elderly adult, and in some jurisdictions, the abuse, neglect, self-neglect, or exploitation of a vulnerable adult; and legal requirements for responding to client dangerousness that may include a duty to warn, report, or treat. Additionally, third-party requests for services, court-ordered treatment, and the counseling of minors bring with them requirements that affect confidentiality. These and any other exceptions to confidentiality mandated by the law in your jurisdiction must be included in each client's informed consent agreement; clients need to understand the limits on the counselor's ability to protect private information before they decide to share it with their counselor *(see Standards A.2.a., A.2.b.)*. Counselors should remain cognizant of the client and counseling contexts likely to trigger requirements for mandatory reporting and exceptions to confidentiality. The most common reporting situations are summarized here.

Reporting Requirements With Minors

Every state has a law requiring a report to the appropriate authorities when a counselor has reason to suspect physical or sexual abuse, or neglect, of a minor *(see Standard B.1.c.)*. Because minors are considered a vulnerable population under the law (individuals who rely on others for their care and well-being), this important limit to confidentiality has been included in the law (Crenshaw

& Lichtenberg, 1993). You should know the relevant law in the jurisdictions in which you practice. Be certain to understand the following facets of the mandatory reporting law: what should be reported, when the report should be made, whether the report should be made by telephone or in writing, and the law's specific definitions of abuse and neglect. Further, many states specify the counselor's responsibilities when the client is presently an adult who reports abuse or neglect that occurred when she or he was a minor. If you work with minors, be familiar with the signs of abuse and neglect, and routinely assess for evidence of abuse or neglect—both current and past—with all of your clients regardless of their presenting difficulties or reason for referral. Most states specify that alleged abuse or neglect must be perpetrated by a caregiver in order to trigger mandatory reporting. Failing to file a mandated report for fear that nothing will be done about it, for fear that a report may just make matters worse, or because you are not certain that your suspicions are valid may very well be a violation of both the law and the *ACA Code of Ethics*. When you suspect the physical or sexual abuse of a minor, file a report in compliance with the laws in your state or province *(see Standard B.1.c.)*.

Reporting Requirements With Elderly or Other Vulnerable Adults

Vulnerable adults are those adults who rely on others for their ongoing care and well-being. This may include the elderly, developmentally disabled persons, or those adults who suffer from an illness or disability that renders them reliant on others for care. If you work with adults, you must be familiar with and careful to adhere to the relevant laws bearing on mandatory reporting in your jurisdiction *(see Standard B.1.c.)* (Welfel, Danzinger, & Santoro, 2000). Assess all of your vulnerable adult and elderly clients for the presence or recent history of physical or sexual abuse, neglect, and, in some jurisdictions, self-neglect or exploitation. You should report even reasonable suspicion of any abuse or neglect to the appropriate agency as specified in your local laws; always file a report within the required time limit and using the format required (e.g., by telephone, in writing).

Dangerousness and the Duty to Warn and Protect

While confidentiality rights protect much of what a client says in counseling, each state and province has implemented laws designed to limit confidentiality when necessary to protect others from harm *(see Standard B.2.a.)*. Most of these laws specify that if a client discloses a specific threat to do imminent harm to an identifiable victim, or group of victims, the counselor has an obligation under the law (*Tarasoff v. Board of Regents of the University of California*, 1976). This obligation typically involves some action on your part to warn, to protect, or both. As a counselor, these reporting laws will typically require you to notify the police and the intended victim of the exact threat and who made it. While most of your clients' expressions of anger, resentment, and hostility will not reach this threshold, you must be prepared to act on any credible threat. If you have a reasonable belief that a client has the potential to act on a threat, you must breach confidentiality—assuming your client does not waive his or her right to confidentiality—to contact the intended victim and the police.

It is important to note that these mandatory reporting laws only apply to threats regarding future violence. Client reports of past violence may not be reported and are protected as confidential information. However, you must act to prevent future harm (Borum & Reddy, 2001).

In some jurisdictions the law allows for an additional option beyond the duty to warn and protect. This additional option is to treat. In general, these jurisdictions offer counselors the opportunity to respond to a client's threat to harm another individual with appropriate counseling intervention. Although the least restrictive form of treatment is typically recommended, don't forget that when a client is at risk of acting on a threat to do lethal harm, inpatient treatment is typically required. In this case, you may have the client involuntarily admitted for inpatient treatment. If the treatment offered effectively prevents the client from acting on threats to harm an individual or group, and if the risk of future harm is no longer clinically significant, you may not be required to warn and protect the threatened person. However, when a counseling plan is ineffective at ameliorating the threat of harm, you must immediately contact the threatened person and police to prevent harm from occurring.

Remember that as a counselor you should be familiar with the warning signs and risk factors for violence and acting-out potential. You should assess for risk of danger to others in every intake interview with a new client, and periodically over time as is appropriate given the nature of each client's clinical problems and behavior. You should conduct a formal risk assessment with all clients who present with any of the risk factors or warning signs for violence (Simon & Tardiff, 2008). Finally, make yourself familiar with the treatment options and resources for managing high-risk clients in your local area; take all threats seriously.

Third-Party Requests for Services

When a client is referred for counseling or for evaluation by a third party, such as an employer, keep in mind that the "client" may be the employer, not the individual being evaluated or counseled. In this case the employer may assume having access to client information or that evaluation results will be forwarded directly to the employer without any access by the individual evaluated *(see Standard B.3.d.)*.

Of course, you must carefully address these expectations with the client in detail during the informed consent agreement. You must ensure that all parties hold an accurate understanding about access to confidential information. It is particularly important that the individual or groups that you counsel or assess understand and agree to such a significant limit on their right to confidentiality.

Court-Ordered Services

Similar to third-party requests for services, court-ordered services by definition alter confidentiality arrangements. When an individual enters the legal system, she or he may lose certain rights. When a court orders an evaluation or treatment, the court, not the individual directly participating in the evaluation or counseling sessions, becomes the counselor's client. Remember to fully disclose these arrangements from the outset of the professional relationship. It is particularly important to ensure that the person(s) receiving services have realistic expectations about who may have access to their confidential information and whether they themselves have such access *(see Standard B.2.c.)*.

Minors

State laws vary in their definitions of a minor; the upper range may be anywhere from 18 to 21 years of age. Further, some states authorize some minors, such as those age 16 and 17, to consent to their own health care in some circumstances. Any individual who legally consents to treatment typically has control over the release of confidential information and may restrict others' access to it.

As a counselor, you should clearly discuss issues of confidentiality with minors as part of the informed consent process, even when a parent or guardian consents to treatment. It is important to ensure that each party understands who will have access to information and the circumstances in which it will be released. In many jurisdictions the parent or guardian of a minor may have the legal right to access to all information shared by the minor in counseling *(see Standards B.5.b., B.5.c.)*. For older minors this may be an untenable situation, and they may not willingly participate in counseling under these circumstances. In these cases, you should work with all parties to reach an agreement on just what types of information may be disclosed to the parent or guardian (e.g., dangerousness to self or other high-risk behaviors) and what information will be kept confidential in the counseling relationship (Barnett, Behnke, Rosenthal, & Koocher, 2007). Keep in mind that the parent or guardian may agree to modify or limit his or her right to access to confidential information from the counseling relationship so the minor can receive needed assistance. You may play a key role in helping them to negotiate this arrangement. But remember, in the end the parent or guardian typically has the final say on this matter; some may wish to assert their right to access to counseling information regardless of the possible impact on the minor's subsequent willingness to participate and share openly.

References

Barnett, J. E., Behnke, S., Rosenthal, S. L., & Koocher, G. P. (2007). In case of ethical dilemma break glass: Commentary on ethical decision making in practice. *Professional Psychology: Research and Practice, 38*, 7–12.

Borum, R., & Reddy, M. (2001). Assessing violence risk in *Tarasoff*-situations: A fact-based model of inquiry. *Behavioral Sciences and the Law, 19*, 375–385.

Crenshaw, W. B., & Lichtenberg, J. W. (1993). Child abuse and the limits of confidentiality: Forewarning practices. *Behavioral Sciences and the Law, 11*, 181–192.

Simon, R. I., & Tardiff, K. (2008). *Textbook of violence assessment and management.* Arlington, VA: American Psychiatric Publishing.

Tarasoff v. Board of Regents of the University of California, Cal. Rptr. 14, No. S.F. 23042 (Cal. S. Ct., 1976).

Welfel, E., Danzinger, P., & Santoro, S. (2000). Mandated reporting of abuse/maltreatment of older adults: A primer for counselors. *Journal of Counseling & Development, 78*, 284–292.

Counseling Suicidal Clients

Sooner or later, nearly every counselor will be faced with a client who is contemplating or actively planning suicide. Suicidal clients naturally generate confusion, anxiety, and even panic among mental health professionals. A wide variety of client circumstances, clinical syndromes, and personality dispositions may heighten the risk of self-harm (Joiner, 2005). Clients who are depressed, abusing substances, or contending with difficult losses or stressors—many of the people you are likely to counsel—are at increased risk for suicide. It is essential that you prepare for client suicidal ideation or behavior in advance. The *ACA Code of Ethics* offers clear guidance with respect to the ethical management of suicidality. Counselors have an overarching ethical duty to protect client welfare, to provide clear informed consent bearing on disclosures of confidential information, and to carefully adhere to both ethical and legal obligations relative to client safety.

When counselors have concerns about a client's suicide risk, they should remember that there are several known *risk factors* for suicide (Jobes, 2006). Although none of these factors alone may predict suicidal behavior, each factor should be considered a potential source of risk, both at the outset of a clinical relationship and periodically as circumstances change or clients become more depressed or impaired. Keep in mind that the absence of these factors does not guarantee that a client is immune to the risk of suicide. When assessing risk of suicide, consider the following risk factors (Barnett & Johnson, 2008; Capuzzi, 2004):

- *Sex:* Men are four times more likely to commit suicide than women.
- *Age:* Elderly people and adolescents are at greater risk.
- *Race:* Caucasians have the highest rates of suicide.

- *Depression:* A history of a mood disorder (e.g., depression, bipolar disorder).
- *Alcohol:* Alcohol abuse or dependence is common.
- *Impulsivity:* A history of impulsive or aggressive behavior.
- *History of attempts:* This greatly increases the likelihood of future attempts.
- *Family history:* Suicide attempts in family or important friends.
- *Chronic illness:* Chronic or serious physical illness or disability.
- *Hopelessness:* Loss of interest or hope in the future.
- *Helplessness:* Feeling that one is unable to change his or her current situation.
- *Loss:* Serious and recent losses.
- *Psychosis:* Serious disorganization or other psychotic symptoms.
- *Social support:* Lack of social support.
- *Plan and means:* An organized plan and access to means raise the risk.

In addition to these general risk factors, there are several *warning signs* of suicide that may manifest in a client's behavior prior to a suicide attempt (Barnett & Johnson, 2008). Again, no single factor predicts a suicide; rather, each factor should raise your concern and prompt further inquiry about potential ideation, intent, and planning. The following are some suicide warning signs:

- *Talking about suicide:* Talking (or writing) about suicide.
- *Verbal cues:* "I wish I were dead. What's the point?"
- *Neglecting self:* Decreased focus on hygiene and appearance.
- *Worsening mood:* Becoming more depressed and hopeless.
- *Sudden loss:* Sudden personal crisis or relational loss.
- *Sudden change in mood:* Dramatic elevation in mood.
- *Suicide planning:* Formulating a plan for suicide.
- *Withdrawal:* Becoming distant and withdrawn from relationships.
- *Preparations:* Giving away belongings, buying a weapon, saving pills.
- *Saying goodbye:* Offering vague thanks or goodbye to friends, family members, or counselor.

In addition to considering the key risk factors and clinical warning signs for suicide, consider each of the following recommendations designed to call attention to essential steps and considerations in keeping clients safe; each recommendation is intended to reduce the overall risk of suicide (Maris, Berman, & Silverman, 2000). Remember that promoting client welfare implies preventing client harm when possible *(see Standard A.1.a.)*.

- Don't hesitate to openly discuss and assess a client's risk to self; asking about suicidal thinking or intent does not cause suicide.
- Assess each new client for suicidal thoughts and intentions regardless of his or her reason for seeking counseling.
- When clients acknowledge suicidal thoughts, take these seriously, create a supportive environment, and conduct a thorough suicide risk assessment.

- Carefully assess a suicidal client's specific ideations related to suicide, any plans, level of intent to carry out the plan, and access to various means for self-harm. Don't forget to inquire about recent losses, previous suicide attempts, and significant models for suicide (e.g., family members, friends, admired celebrities).
- Provide clients with a clear picture of the limits to confidentiality during the informed consent process; when clients are at risk for suicide, periodically revisit these limitations *(see Standards A.2.a., A.2.b., B.1.d.)*.
- Ensure that clients understand your obligation as a counselor to protect them from "serious and foreseeable harm" *(see Standard B.2.a.)*.
- Always make yourself familiar with legal requirements bearing on mandatory reporting of suicidal clients and limits to confidentiality in your jurisdiction *(see Standard B.2.a.)*.
- Make sure that you are competent to assess suicidality before engaging in any independent counseling work; develop specialized competence in suicide risk assessment if you plan to work with high-risk populations such as those with mood, substance abuse, or chronic medical disorders.
- Pursue education, training, and supervision in suicide risk assessment and crisis intervention strategies.
- Periodically consider the suicide risk for each of your clients.
- In addition to subjective assessments such as clinical interviews, utilize questionnaires and rating forms that provide a more objective assessment. Further, these may be repeated over the course of counseling to track progress or deterioration in the client's functioning.
- When working with high-risk clients, seriously consider consultation with colleagues with demonstrated expertise in this area.
- When supervising other counselors, remember to protect the client's welfare first and foremost *(see Standard F.1.a.)*, ensure that clients understand the limitations to confidentiality related to suicide risk *(see Standard F.1.c.)*, and be certain that your supervisees understand emergency procedures—including ways to contact you—related to responding to client suicidality *(see Standard F.4.b.)*.
- When you identify a client as at risk for suicide, be sure to tailor the treatment plan to the client's level of risk; consider more frequent appointments or inpatient admission when this is appropriate.
- When obtaining a "no-harm" contract from suicidal clients in which they guarantee not to harm themselves before seeking help from you or another provider, recognize that no-harm contracts may not prevent a suicide or protect you from legal repercussions. Timely and thorough risk assessments and effective ongoing treatment are the best ways to assist clients.
- Be familiar with policies and practices related to both voluntary and involuntary psychiatric admission in your area; routinely consult with a psychiatrist or other provider with inpatient admission privileges.
- Make sure suicidal clients know exactly how to contact you or an appropriate colleague, answering service, or emergency room.

- Clearly document the client's mental status, your ongoing risk assessments, and a rationale for diagnostic and treatment plan decisions in the client's record.
- Consider providing suicidal outpatient clients with contact information to the National Suicide Prevention Lifeline (www.suicidepreventionlifeline.org) and other suicide hotlines as a backup to your own contact information.
- Remain aware of your own reactions to suicide and suicidal clients; recognize that working with suicidal clients is stressful for most counselors. Seek appropriate consultation, engage in self-care, and to the extent indicated, limit the number of suicidal clients with whom you work.
- Be particularly cautious about referring, transferring, or terminating with a client who has been or is currently suicidal; take extra care to ensure that this transition goes smoothly and that the client does not feel abandoned in the process.

References

Barnett, J. E., & Johnson, W. B. (2008). *Ethics desk reference for psychologists.* Washington, DC: American Psychological Association.

Capuzzi, D. C. (Ed.). (2004). *Suicide across the life span.* Washington, DC: American Counseling Association.

Jobes, D. A. (2006). *Managing suicidal risk: A collaborative approach.* New York: Guilford Press.

Joiner, T. E. (2005). *Why people die by suicide.* Cambridge, MA: Harvard University Press.

Maris, R. W., Berman, A. L., & Silverman, M. M. (2000). Treatment and prevention of suicide. In R. W. Maris, A. L. Berman, & M. M. Silverman (Eds.), *Comprehensive textbook of suicidology* (pp. 509–535). New York: Guilford Press.

Boundaries and Multiple Relationships in Counseling

Counselors work to develop relationships with clients that are rooted in caring and based on trust. In every counseling relationship, counselors help clients to achieve their goals while minimizing the risk of exploitation or harm *(see Standard A.4.a.)*. Maintaining appropriate boundaries and exercising caution when entering more than one relationship with a client are ways that counselors can help to prevent harm.

Boundaries are the ground rules of the professional relationship (Smith & Fitzpatrick, 1995). Boundaries afford a structure or framework within which a counseling relationship can thrive. Boundaries have to do with the contours of a relationship and include variables such as meeting location, meeting duration, physical touch, gift-giving, and reciprocity of personal disclosure. At times, a boundary may be crossed (e.g., extending a session, touching a grieving client on the forearm, sharing personal information, conducting a home visit) in a way that is clinically appropriate, relevant to the client's counseling plan, and helpful to the client. When a boundary crossing is inconsistent with the client's counseling needs, does not meet professional standards, and is likely to be harmful to a client, it is a *boundary violation* (Gutheil & Gabbard, 1998). Boundary violations are often motivated by the counselor's needs and not by the client's best interests (e.g., touching a client in a sexual manner, meeting with a client after hours for romantic reasons, extending session time limits without a clear clinical rationale, disclosing personal information for the purpose of eliciting emotional care or intimacy from a client). It is important to note that rigid adherence to boundaries (e.g., never touching a client under any circumstances, refusing every small gift, refusing to extend a session for any reason) may be just as harmful to a client and the counseling relationship as a boundary violation (Lazarus & Zur, 2002).

Multiple relationships involve engaging in more than one kind of relationship with a client, for instance, serving as a counselor while simultaneously serving as a close friend, employer, or coworker. The *ACA Code of Ethics* is clear that multiple relationships often place clients at risk of harm and increase the risk of exploitation and other negative consequences *(see Standard A.5.)*. However, not all multiple relationships are necessarily harmful; Standards A.5.c. and A.5.d. emphasize the possibility of clients benefiting from certain kinds of multiple relationships. For instance, attending a client's wedding ceremony, purchasing a product or service from a former client, and maintaining membership in a community or professional association in which a client is also a member may afford a client certain therapeutic benefits (Barnett, 1999). Keep in mind that the burden to demonstrate that a multiple relationship benefits and does not harm a client is exclusively the counselor's.

Here are several suggestions for counselors to consider before embarking on more than one relationship with a client, student, or research participant.

Key Multiple Relationship Questions

Prior to crossing a client boundary or entering a second kind of relationship with an existing client, ask yourself the following questions:

- Is the new role consistent with the client's counseling needs and not motivated by my own interests?
- Is there any chance that crossing this boundary or entering a new relationship could lead to exploitation or harm to the client?
- What are the likely risks and benefits to the client?
- Could participation in the new relationship impair my objectivity or judgment?
- Is participation in this specific kind of multiple relationship consistent with prevailing professional standards and with the *ACA Code of Ethics*?
- Has the client consented to the boundary crossing or multiple relationship?
- Is the multiple relationship, and my rationale for embarking on it, clearly documented in the client record?
- Would a jury of my peers likely concur that this boundary crossing or multiple role was clearly in my client's best interests?
- If the potential risks and benefits of the multiple relationship remain unclear, have I consulted with appropriate colleagues or an ethics committee?

Be Cautious About Bartering

Bartering involves the exchange of goods or services for counseling. Because not all clients have the financial means to access counseling services, counselors might consider accepting a client's goods or services for counseling services. When bartering with clients, it is essential to consider the following:

- Consult Standard A.10.d.
- Ensure that clients will not be exploited or harmed as a result of the exchange.
- Always discuss the exchange openly with your client to ensure that the barter agreement feels equitable.
- Periodically initiate discussion of the barter agreement to ensure that it continues to be fair from the client's perspective.
- When in doubt about the relative value of a good or service or the advisability of agreeing to a bartering exchange with a client, seek consultation from a colleague.
- Be especially cautious when bartering services because their value may be more difficult to determine and dissatisfaction with the quality or services provided may occur for both counselor and client.

Think Carefully About Accepting Gifts

Nowhere is the significance of boundaries more clearly evident than in the decision to give or receive gifts from a client. Accepting a gift of homemade artwork from a child client, baked goods at holiday time, or the offer of food from a client during a home visit may be therapeutic and consistent with the client's best interests. Refusing a gift may prove harmful to a client and inconsistent with respect for certain cultural norms. But accepting gifts must be done carefully and with regard for the potential for exploitation or violations of appropriate boundaries (Herlihy & Corey, 2006). Accepting expensive gifts should generally be avoided. Before accepting a gift, remember to:

- Consult Standard A.10.e.
- Consider whose needs are being served by giving or receiving a gift.
- Ensure that you have not done something to suggest that a gift is in order.
- Ask yourself whether the gift is of such a magnitude that it may impair your objectivity or judgment.
- Consider relevant cultural factors when interpreting the meaning of a gift.
- Ask yourself whether you are comfortable documenting and having colleagues learn about the gift you have accepted.

Do Not Solicit Client Testimonials

By their very nature, testimonial endorsements by current or former clients—used in the counselor's advertising efforts—constitute a multiple relationship with the client. Because client testimonials purely benefit the counselor and cannot be construed as motivated by the client's best interests, testimonials result in exploitive multiple relationships. The *ACA Code of Ethics* leaves no doubt that you must not solicit testimonials from current or former clients *(see Standard C.3.b.)*.

Romantic and Sexual Relationships With Clients Are Always Off Limits

The *ACA Code of Ethics* makes it crystal clear that sexual or romantic relationships with current clients *(Standard A.5.a.)*, students *(Standard F.10.a.)*, supervisees *(Standard F.3.b.)*, research participants *(Standard G.3.b.)*, and others closely associated with them are always likely to cause harm and are therefore prohibited. Sexual and romantic roles with those we serve professionally take advantage of the trust placed in counselors by members of the public; they nearly always result in exploitation (Herlihy & Corey, 2006). When sexual or romantic feelings about a client, student, supervisee, or research participant arise, engage in the following steps:

- Recognize that sexual feelings in counseling or supervision are normal; most mental health professionals report this experience from time to time.
- Accept the fact that you may not enter a romantic or sexual relationship with a current client, supervisee, student, or research participant.
- Accept that you may not consider beginning a romantic or sexual relationship with a former client until at least 5 years have elapsed from the date of your last professional contact, and that even after the 5-year moratorium, the burden of demonstrating that this new role is not exploitive or harmful rests on your shoulders.
- Before engaging in a romantic or sexual relationship with a former student, supervisee, or research participant, carefully consider the risk of exploitation and harm to the person who may remain at a relative power disadvantage.
- Always seek collegial consultation when experiencing these feelings or when you are considering such a relationship with a former client or student.
- Remember that as a general rule, romantic and sexual relationships with those you have previously served as a counselor are always risky and likely to result in exploitation or harm.

References

Barnett, J. E. (1999). Multiple relationships: Ethical dilemmas and practical solutions. In L. VandeCreek & T. Jackson (Eds.), *Innovations in clinical practice* (pp. 255–267). Sarasota, FL: Professional Resource Press.

Gutheil, T. G., & Gabbard, G. O. (1998). Misuses and misunderstandings of boundary theory in clinical and regulatory settings. *American Journal of Psychiatry, 155,* 409–414.

Herlihy, B., & Corey, G. (2006). *Boundary issues in counseling: Multiple roles and responsibilities* (2nd ed.). Alexandria, VA: American Counseling Association.

Lazarus, A. A., & Zur, O. (2002). *Dual relationships in psychotherapy.* New York: Springer.

Smith, D., & Fitzpatrick, M. (1995). Patient–therapist boundary issues: An integrative review of theory and research. *Professional Psychology: Research and Practice, 26,* 499–506.

Competence

Counselors aspire to provide high-quality services to their clients. To do so, counselors establish and maintain relevant competence so that clients receive the highest level of counseling services possible. Think of competence as comprising the knowledge, skills, attitudes, and values needed to effectively provide counseling services to a specific client in a specific context (McLeod, 1996). Counselors obtain knowledge through formal course work and educational experiences, skills through practical course work and supervised counseling experiences, and attitudes and values through both training experiences and modeling from faculty, supervisors, and mentors. Genuine competence hinges on the values espoused in the *ACA Code of Ethics.* The ability to effectively implement or apply requisite knowledge, attitudes, and skills in a competent manner is dependent on each counselor's character and emotional functioning. Interference or impairment in either of these areas can have a detrimental impact on competence regardless of one's level of knowledge or skill. Thus, consistent with the introduction of Section C: Professional Responsibility of the *ACA Code of Ethics,* each counselor must attend to his or her own emotional, physical, mental, and spiritual well-being so as to provide competent and effective counseling services *(see also Standard C.2.g.).*

Counselors striving for competence must attend to, monitor, and at times address a number of issues bearing on the delivery of excellent services. Here are several key considerations for establishing and maintaining professional competence.

The Competence Continuum

Competence is not a unitary concept. You are not necessarily either competent or incompetent. Competence exists on a continuum. Your ethical obligation is to actively work to maintain the highest standards of competence possible. While minimal standards of competence exist, and they should always be exceeded, it is important to aspire to the highest standards of competence possible in all your counseling activities and roles (McLeod, 1996).

Scope of Competence

You may be competent in one area or aspect of counseling and not in another. Competence is not a global construct. Each aspect of your counseling practice must be actively assessed to ensure sufficient competence. Just because you are competent in one aspect of counseling (e.g., childhood disorders, posttrauma counseling) does not guarantee that you are competent in other areas (e.g., psychological testing, counseling with older adults).

Competence Over Time

Competence is fluid, not static; competence at one point in time does not guarantee competence at a later date. Once you develop competence in a particular area of counseling, you must take active steps to maintain competence. Failure to seek out ongoing education, training, supervision, consultation, or other professional development activities may result in a degradation of your level of initial competence. Actively participate in ongoing continuing education to maintain and expand your competence as a counselor *(see Standard C.2.f.)*.

Changes in the Profession

The scientific knowledge base of the counseling profession is constantly changing. New research findings regularly move the counseling field forward. Failure to remain aware of new findings and to integrate them into your counseling practice, and neglecting additional training, may limit your competence. As the counseling field evolves, keep up with changes and innovations; continually update your knowledge and skills.

Scientific Basis for Decisions

Remember to base your counseling decisions, and the use of all assessment and treatment techniques and strategies, on empirically derived findings or findings that are grounded in widely accepted theories *(see Standard C.6.e.)*. Failure to do so can place clients at risk and could lead to harm. Exercise great care when using unproven techniques with clients and clearly describe them as experimental to clients *(see Standards A.4.a., C.6.e.)*.

Multicultural Competence

Failure to attend to the full range of client diversity and how individual differences are relevant to client counseling needs may have a negative impact on competence *(see Standards A.2.c., A.4.b., E.5.b.)* (Barnett & Polakoff, 2000). Be sensitive to, aware of, and knowledgeable about the many diversity-related factors that will affect the counseling relationship and process *(see Standards C.2.a., C.2.f.)*. For example, competence in the assessment and treatment of depression is important for counselors, yet failing to appreciate how depression may be experienced or displayed by different age groups, and by members of different cultural or ethnic groups, would severely limit competence with a range of clients (Leung & Barnett, 2008).

Monitoring Competence

You are responsible for monitoring your own competence on an ongoing basis. This should be an active process of self-assessment and should include consultation with colleagues when you are unsure whether you possess the needed competence to provide services in a particular area of counseling practice *(see Standard C.2.e.)*.

Scope of Counseling Practice

No counselor can be competent with all counseling skills and techniques, client populations and settings, and counseling modalities. You must develop the knowledge, skills, and other abilities needed to competently and effectively provide specific counseling services to particular clients (e.g., children, adults, families), in particular settings (e.g., outpatient, inpatient, schools), with particular modalities (e.g., individual, couples, group), and using specific techniques *(see Standard C.2.a.)* (Epstein & Hundert, 2002). Work to develop the specialized competence required in each facet of your professional work *(see Standard C.2.b.)*.

Specialized Competence

Develop a broad range of competencies to include those needed in assessment, treatment, supervision, teaching, and research. Recognize that each of these may require some different and specialized knowledge and skills, and obtain the needed competence for effective counseling practice in each of these areas *(see Standards E.2.a., E.5.a., F.2.a., F.6.a.)*.

Limits of Competence

Monitor your clients' counseling needs and the effectiveness of your counseling services on an ongoing basis. When it becomes clear that a client's counseling needs exceed your competence, it is important that you develop the competence needed to effectively treat your client, or if that is not possible, refer the client to a counselor or other professional who possesses the requisite competence to best meet the client's counseling needs *(see Standards A.11.b., C.2.d.)*.

Self-Care and Competence

Because the many stresses and demands of your personal and professional life affect your ability to provide competent counseling services, you must monitor your emotional, mental, physical, and spiritual functioning on an ongoing basis (Baker, 2003). Practicing ongoing self-care is essential to maintaining competence as a counselor *(see Section C, Introduction; Standard C.2.g.)*. Failure to take adequate care of yourself may result in impaired counseling competence, having a detrimental effect on your clients (Norcross & Guy, 2007). Continuing to provide services when your competence is impaired violates the *ACA Code of Ethics (see Standards A.4.a., C.2.g.)*. When distressed or unsure of your ability to practice competently, consult with a knowledgeable and trusted colleague or professional ethics committee *(see Standard C.2.e.)*.

Employment Decisions

When making employment decisions, only accept positions for which you possess the competence to fulfill the job requirements in an ethical and competent manner *(see Standard C.2.c.)*. The fact that a particular role (e.g., supervising trainees) is a part of one's job description is not a sufficient justification for providing that particular counseling service in the absence of established competence *(see Standards A.4.a., C.2.a., C.2.c.)*.

References

Baker, E. K. (2003). *Caring for ourselves: A therapist's guide to personal and professional well-being.* Washington, DC: American Psychological Association.

Barnett, J. E., & Polakoff, N. (2000). Maintaining competence in the new millennium. In L. VandeCreek & T. Jackson (Eds.), *Innovations in clinical practice* (pp. 257–272). Sarasota, FL: Professional Resources Press.

Epstein, R. M., & Hundert, E. M. (2002). Defining and assessing professional competence. *Journal of the American Medical Association, 287*, 226–235.

Leung, C. Y. Y., & Barnett, J. E. (2008). Multicultural assessment and ethical practice. *The Independent Practitioner, 28*, 139–143.

McLeod, J. (1996). Counselor competence. In R. Bayne, I. Horton, & J. Bimrose (Eds.), *New directions in counseling* (pp. 37–47). New York: Routledge.

Norcross, J. C., & Guy, J. D. (2007). *Leaving it at the office: A guide to psychotherapist self-care.* New York: Guilford Press.

Supervision

Supervision is an essential aspect of every counselor's training and professional development. Counselors-in-training apply what they learn in course work in practicum and internship settings under the watchful eye of a more experienced supervisor. Supervisory feedback is often invaluable for practical learning of the counseling process. Counselors who accept the role of counseling supervisor must recognize that this role brings with it a number of obligations. Ultimately, the quality of supervision may have a direct impact on the quality of counseling services delivered through supervisees to clients. Additionally, supervisors are responsible for their supervisees' training and professional development. Taking on a supervisee is a significant responsibility. It should not be taken lightly or regarded as just another collateral obligation. Counselor supervisors must ensure that they dedicate sufficient time to this role so that supervisees' and their clients' needs are competently addressed.

To ensure that the counseling supervision process is a positive and beneficial one for counseling supervisees and their clients alike, here are several suggestions that are rooted in the relevant sections of the *ACA Code of Ethics.*

Competence

Prior to entering the role of counseling supervisor, ensure that you possess the requisite competencies to effectively serve in this role *(see Standard F.2.a.)*. Remember that you should work to achieve two separate but related types of competence. First, ensure that you are competent in all areas of counseling that you plan to supervise, such as particular assessment and treatment techniques.

Examples include individual, group, or family counseling or achievement testing in children. Competence in one area does not necessarily make a counselor competent in another. Second, seek competence in supervision itself. This involves obtaining needed education and training in conducting supervision, and understanding the developmental processes of counselors-in-training. Such preparation will ideally include supervision of your supervision.

Informed Consent

At the outset of the supervisory relationship, provide supervisees with fully informed consent to the supervisory relationship *(see Standard F.4.a.)*. This should include expectations for both supervisor and supervisee, meeting schedules, any fees involved, the process of evaluation and feedback *(see Standard F.5.a.)*, emergency procedures and contact information *(see Standard F.4.b.)*, ethical and legal standards and responsibilities *(see Standard F.4.c.)*, and policies and procedures for the ending of the supervisory relationship *(see Standard F.4.d.)*.

Assessing Training Needs

Before allowing a supervisee to see his or her first client, first assess the supervisee's current level of competence and specific training needs. This will help to ensure that each supervisee receives needed training, that the supervision experience is tailored to the supervisee's strengths and weaknesses, and that the welfare of the supervisee's clients is appropriately safeguarded.

Intensity of Supervision

Supervision occurs along a developmental continuum. The supervision you provide to a counseling supervisee will by necessity be more intense at early stages of professional development when greater guidance and oversight are needed. As the supervisee develops and counseling skills are enhanced, you may provide less active supervision. For instance, milestones in the progression of developmental supervision might include sitting in on the counseling session with the supervisee and client (live in-person supervision), providing live supervision from behind a one-way mirror with feedback and suggestions shared by electronic means, reviewing video- or audiotapes of counseling sessions prior to supervision sessions, and finally, review of the supervisee's documentation of counseling sessions, using this as the basis for discussion in supervision. Of course, a combination of these approaches should be used as is warranted by your supervisee's competence level and rate of development.

Representation to Clients

Actively ensure that supervisees do not misrepresent themselves to clients as independent counseling service providers. Ensure that each client is informed of the supervisee counselor's training status, the identity of the supervisor, and the impact of supervision on the counseling process as part of the informed consent agreement. Be sure that supervisees only use recording equipment after clients understand the purpose of recording and provide their informed consent *(see Standard F.1.c.)*.

Attention to Ethical and Legal Issues

Be certain that your supervisees are aware of all relevant ethics standards and laws that regulate the practice of counseling *(see Standard F.4.c.)*. Further, integrate these issues into all aspects of supervision as is relevant and model ethical counseling practice for your supervisees (Bernard & Goodyear, 2008).

Attention to Diversity Issues

Integrate diversity into all aspects of supervision to ensure that supervisees develop a thoughtful and caring approach in their counseling of all clients *(see Standard F.2.b.)* (D'Andrea & Daniels, 1997). Communicate clearly that multiculturalism and attention to all aspects of diversity is an integral part of the counseling and supervision processes. Ensure that all assessments, diagnostic formulations, counseling treatment, and supervision itself are sensitive to the wide range of diversity that your supervisees may encounter (Ancis & Ladany, 2001).

Boundaries and Multiple Relationships

Remain cognizant of the imbalance of power present in the supervisory relationship. Strive to focus on the supervisee's best interests, and do not take advantage of a supervisee's natural dependence and naiveté. Nonprofessional relationships with supervisees are undertaken cautiously and only when consistent with the supervisees' training needs *(see Standard F.3.a., F.3.e.)*. Do not provide supervision to individuals with whom you have preexisting close relationships, such as friends, romantic partners, or close relatives *(see Standard F.3.d.)*. Because of the great potential for harm, you must never enter sexual or romantic relationships with supervisees *(see Standard F.3.b.)* (Kitchener, 1988). For similar reasons, do not provide counseling services to supervisees, but instead make appropriate referrals when such services are needed or requested *(see Standard F.5.c.)*.

Supervisor as Gatekeeper

As a counseling supervisor, you have responsibilities to the counseling profession, to supervisees' current clients, and to their future clients as well (Whiston & Emerson, 1989). Through active oversight and supervision, you are obligated to monitor each supervisee's conduct, competence, and ongoing professional development. When difficulties become evident, keep in mind that you bear an important responsibility for ensuring that supervisees receive needed intervention and remediation, and assist them to obtain needed remedial assistance *(see Standard F.5.b.)*. When such efforts are not successful, recommend dismissal from the supervisee's training program and document your decision as well as all efforts to assist the supervisee *(see Standard F.5.b.)*. Refuse to endorse counseling supervisees for completion of training requirements, licensure, or certification when you deem them not competent or fit to provide counseling services *(see Standard F.5.d.)*.

Supervisor as Role Model

In addition to the important didactic and supervisory roles you embody in counseling supervision, you must also accept the great responsibility to serve as a role model to supervisees. Supervisees will view their supervisors' conduct as indicative of what one should expect from a professional counselor (Gray, Ladany, Walker, & Ancis, 2001). Keep in mind that supervisees are often influenced more by what they see and experience first hand—your behavior—than by what they are told.

References

Ancis, J. R., & Ladany, N. (2001). A multicultural framework for counselor supervision. In L. J. Bradley & N. Ladany (Eds.), *Counselor supervision: Principles, process, and practice* (3rd ed., pp. 63–90). Philadelphia: Brunner-Routledge.

Bernard, J. M., & Goodyear, R. K. (2008). *Fundamentals of clinical supervision.* Boston: Allyn & Bacon.

D'Andrea, M., & Daniels, J. (1997). Multicultural counseling supervision: Central issues, theoretical considerations, and practical strategies. In D. B. Pope-Davis & C. Hardin (Eds.), *Multicultural counseling competencies: Assessment, education and training, and supervision* (pp. 290–309). Thousand Oaks, CA: Sage.

Gray, L. A., Ladany, N., Walker, J. A., & Ancis, J. R. (2001). Psychotherapy trainees' experiences of counterproductive events in supervision. *Journal of Counseling Psychology, 48,* 371–383.

Kitchener, K. S. (1988). Dual role relationships: What makes them so problematic? *Journal of Counseling & Development, 67,* 217–221.

Whiston, S. C., & Emerson, S. (1989). Ethical implications for supervisors in counseling of trainees. *Counselor Education and Supervision, 28,* 319–325.

Managed Care

The health care industry has undergone significant changes in recent years. In response to increasing costs and reported concerns over inappropriate utilization patterns, there have been a number of efforts to reduce the costs of health care. Managed care developed as one such effort to reduce costs and exert greater control over utilization patterns (Barnett, 1997).

Managed care refers to a range of insurance entities that provide oversight of the utilization of health insurance to pay for needed health care. It may take the form of health maintenance organizations, preferred provider organizations, and other forms. The essential feature is that each participant's insurance benefits are "managed." This means that one may only access health care services if they are approved by utilization review personnel who are employed by the insurer and who use the insurance company's criteria for determining if the requested treatment meets the insurer's standards for medically necessary treatment. Additionally, insurers may include limits on covered treatments in one's policy. Examples include limiting outpatient counseling and psychotherapy to a maximum number of visits per year (e.g., 10 or 20) and inpatient treatment to a certain maximum number of days per year regardless of diagnosis or severity of symptoms (e.g., 30 days), only offering insurance coverage for certain conditions or types of treatment and not others (e.g., individual counseling but not couples counseling; anxiety and depression but not personality disorders), and excluding all preexisting conditions.

While managed care may help reduce some health care costs (costs to the insurance company), it also can bring with it a number of challenges and dilemmas that counselors must be prepared to confront and address to ensure their ethical practice (Glosoff, Garcia, Herlihy, & Remley, 1999). Issues to be addressed here include informed consent, confidentiality and its limits, competence, contracts, utilization review, and termination and abandonment. Attention to each of these issues should assist counselors to provide care to their clients in a managed care environment in compliance with the *ACA Code of Ethics* and in keeping with their clients' best interests.

Informed Consent

As is clearly stated in the *ACA Code of Ethics (see Standard A.2., Informed Consent in the Counseling Relationship)*, counselors always obtain their clients' fully informed consent prior to providing any professional counseling services. Clients have the right to know all information that might reasonably impact their decision to participate in the counseling services before the services are provided. The following are some questions clients may have that relate to the informed consent process in counseling when managed care is involved:

- Are these counseling services covered by my insurance?
- Are you a participating provider, and if not, will my insurance cover the counseling services you provide?
- Do I have to pay a copayment or is everything covered by the insurance?
- Does my insurance place any limits on the length of treatment or type of treatment I can receive?
- Do I have to receive a diagnosis to have my counseling covered by my insurance?
- Are there any restrictions based on preexisting conditions or the type of counseling treatment I need?
- Are there any limits to the amount of counseling I can receive through my insurance?
- Is everything we discuss confidential?

Counselors should ensure that clients have all relevant information from the outset of the counseling relationship so that clients can make an informed decision about participating. All points mentioned in Standard A.2.b., Types of Information Needed (in Informed Consent), should also be addressed. Those of particular relevance to counseling in managed care include counseling techniques to be used and any potential limitations to counseling services to be provided; the counselor's qualifications, credentials, and relevant experience; the implications of diagnosis; confidentiality and any potential limits to confidentiality; and fees and billing arrangements.

Confidentiality and Its Limits

Although most counseling clients will anticipate that the information they share with their counselor will be kept confidential (Miller & Thelen, 1986), in fact, there are limits to confidentiality when one participates in managed care. The utilization review process (discussed further below) often necessitates that the counselor share detailed information about clients and their counseling treatment to obtain authorization for insurance coverage for counseling services provided (Barnett, 1997). Knowing the nature and extent of information to be shared with the insurance company from the outset may affect many clients' willingness to participate in treatment or, at a minimum, may affect what they decide to share with their counselor.

In an effort to help address these concerns, Keith-Spiegel and Koocher (1985) recommended that the following paragraph be included in all informed consent agreements when managed care is involved:

> If you choose to use your coverage, I shall have to file a form with the company telling them when our appointments were and what services I performed (i.e., psychotherapy, consultation, or evaluation). I will also have to formulate a diagnosis and advise the company of that. The company claims to keep this information confidential, although I have no control over the information once it leaves my office. If you have questions about this you may wish to check with the company providing the coverage. You may certainly choose to pay for my services out-of-pocket and avoid the use of insurance altogether, if you wish. (p. 76)

Competence

In their efforts to reduce counseling costs, managed care companies may place restrictions on the types of counseling services they authorize. Cost containment measures may place an emphasis on the provision of brief individual counseling services and group counseling services. While these forms of counseling may be appropriate for many clients, it is essential that counselors possess the needed competence (through education, training, and supervised counseling experience) to effectively provide these services.

Some managed care companies may require participating counselors to accept all clients who are referred to them by the managed care company. Such a requirement would place great demands on the counselor's competence. An argument can easily be made that no counselor could possess the knowledge and skills needed to meet the counseling needs of every client with whom he or she comes in contact. Referrals to other mental health professionals should be made when a client's needs exceed the counselor's areas of competence, and care should be taken when agreeing to participate in managed care.

Contracts

Managed care companies may have unrealistic expectations of participating counselors. Examples include accepting all referrals, providing 24-hour emergency coverage and meeting with all clients within a specified time period, agreeing to only use certain counseling treatment modalities, and agreeing to grant the managed care company's personnel access to all client records at any time. It may be unrealistic for counselors to expect to meet some of these contractual requirements. Other requirements will be inconsistent with the standards of the *ACA Code of Ethics*. Accordingly, it is essential that counselors read all contracts carefully to be sure they understand what they are agreeing to. It is further recommended that counselors seek expert legal counsel prior to signing contracts.

Utilization Review

The utilization review process is used by managed care companies to ensure that all services provided are needed and covered by the client's policy. The informed consent agreement with clients should address the role of utilization review because of limits that may be placed on counseling services authorized and because of the sensitive information about the client that may be shared with utilization review personnel.

The utilization review process may also create a conflict-of-interest situation for counselors. In their effort to ensure that clients obtain needed services, it may be tempting for counselors to alter a client's diagnosis, exaggerate the severity of symptoms, or overstate treatment needs. While advocating for clients is an important role for counselors, honesty in the utilization review process is essential.

Termination and Abandonment

Managed care may place restrictions on counseling services that are authorized for clients through either annual contractual limits, the utilization review process, or both (Danzinger & Welfel, 2001). This has implications for treatment goals that are agreed to and for how the counseling process is planned. For example, it would be inappropriate to agree to long-term treatment goals for a client whose insurance only covers 10 sessions annually.

Even if a client's insurance contract appears to offer coverage, the contract is often worded with phrases such as "up to 50 sessions per year." The "up to" is then regulated through the utilization review process. A counselor and client may be moving forward to their agreed-upon counseling goals and then managed care personnel may deny authorization for any further counseling. Counselors should appeal all such adverse utilization review decisions (see *Wickline v. State of California*, 1986) and continue providing any clinically indicated counseling rather than immediately terminating counseling. Then, pending the outcome of the appeal, the counselor can decide on the appropriate course of action keeping in mind the client's best interests (see the next chapter, Termination and Abandonment, for additional guidance).

References

Barnett, J. E. (1997). Why managed care? *Psychotherapy in Private Practice, 16*, 1–14.

Danzinger, P. R., & Welfel, E. R. (2001). The impact of managed care on mental health counselors: A survey of perceptions, practices and compliance with ethical standards. *Journal of Mental Health Counseling, 23*, 137–150.

Glosoff, H. L., Garcia, J., Herlihy, B., & Remley, T. P. (1999). Managed care: Ethical considerations for counselors. *Counseling and Values, 44*, 8–16.
Keith-Spiegel, P., & Koocher, G. P. (1985). *Ethics in psychology.* New York: Random House.
Miller, D. J., & Thelen, M. H. (1986). Knowledge and beliefs about confidentiality in psychotherapy. *Professional Psychology: Research and Practice, 17,* 15–19.
Wickline v. State of California, 192 Cal. App. 3d 1630 (1986).

Termination and Abandonment

The counseling relationship may end for a variety of reasons. These may include client-motivated reasons and counselor-motivated reasons.

Client-Motivated Reasons for Termination

Client-motivated reasons for ending the counseling relationship include the following.

Client's Goals Are Achieved

The client's counseling goals have been achieved and both counselor and client agree that termination is appropriate. While this is perhaps the most desired type of counseling termination, it often does not occur; be prepared for the other reasons for termination.

Insurance Benefits Are Exhausted

Many clients utilize their health insurance to at least partially pay for counseling. When insurance benefits are exhausted, many clients may be unable to afford counseling, at least not at the original fee. Counselors who fail to anticipate and help clients to plan for this possibility may place clients' welfare in jeopardy.

Financial Limitations

A client's financial situation may change, perhaps because of losing a job or experiencing unplanned expenses, rendering the client unable to afford continued counseling. Counselors should consider alternative arrangements that best meet the client's ongoing counseling needs.

Moving From the Area

A client may move from the local area for a variety of reasons. At times, relocations are anticipated—offering opportunity for client–counselor planning—whereas at other times, relocations may be abrupt. Counselors should provide assistance with the referral process while supporting clients through this transition.

Transferring to a New Counselor

Clients may decide to transfer to a new counselor because of dissatisfaction with their current counseling, changes in their counseling needs, limitations in your abilities, or a simple desire for a change. Counselors must always respond to such requests for transfer in a manner that is respectful and in concert with the client's best interests.

Dropping Out of Counseling

At times, clients may simply discontinue counseling. They may miss an appointment or cancel an appointment and then fail to respond to a follow-up phone call or letter. In these situations, counselors must respect the right of the client to discontinue services while offering to provide referrals or continued care in the future if the client wishes to continue at a later date.

Counselor-Motivated Reasons for Termination

Counselor-motivated reasons for ending the counseling relationship include the following.

Counselor Competence Issues

You may find that as a counseling relationship evolves or as new problems are revealed, a client's counseling needs may exceed your areas of competence. This may prompt you to make referrals to other mental health or medical professionals who possess the competencies needed to effectively meet the client's counseling needs *(see Standards A.11.b., C.2.a., C.2.d.)*.

Lack of Client Progress

When, despite your best efforts, it becomes clear that a client is not benefiting from counseling, you may decide that the client's best interests dictate a transfer to a different counseling professional *(see Standard A.11.c.)*.

Boundary Issues and Multiple Relationships

Should you discover that a potentially harmful or ethically problematic multiple relationship or boundary crossing has occurred or is likely to occur with a client, transferring the client to a new counselor may be warranted *(see Standards*

A.4.a., A.5.a., A.5.c., A.5.d.). If you are unsure whether a particular boundary crossing or multiple relationship is inappropriate or contraindicated, seek consultation with an experienced colleague *(see Standard C.2.e.).*

Conflicts or Threats

If you experience significant conflicts with a client or if a client threatens you, is assaultive, or is stalking you, you will likely find that effectively continuing the counseling relationship is not possible. In this case transferring the client to another counseling professional or treatment facility becomes necessary *(see Standard A.11.c.).*

Lack of Counselor Availability

At times, a client's counseling needs may be greater than your availability. For example, if you have a small part-time practice and many other obligations that place demands on your time, working with suicidal clients may be beyond your ability to deliver the appropriate level of care; acutely impaired clients will be more effectively treated by colleagues with greater availability.

Counselor Illness, Disability, or Death

You may find that personal health factors one day interfere with your ability to meet your clients' counseling needs. In these situations you may need to cut back or withdraw from counseling practice and refer clients to colleagues who may better be able to meet clients' ongoing needs *(see Standard C.2.g.).* While your own death may not be pleasant to think about, planning ahead so that your clients' counseling needs are addressed is of great importance. You should plan in advance for illness, disability, and death and arrange for a colleague to serve as a records custodian and arrange for client referrals and transfers of care should these be needed *(see Standard C.2.h.).*

Counselor Retirement

At some point you may decide to retire from counseling practice. When doing so, you should provide clients with adequate notice, make referrals as needed to ensure that their counseling needs are appropriately addressed, and arrange for a colleague to maintain counseling records so former clients may have access to them as needed in the future *(see Standard C.2.h.).*

End of a Training Experience

Every training experience ends at some time for every counselor-in-training. Counselors in training programs should discuss this fact from the outset of the counseling relationship and help clients plan accordingly. For those clients who require or request ongoing counseling, a transition period including transfer to another counseling professional should occur with the support and assistance of the counselor-in-training.

Recommendations for Terminating the Counseling Relationship

Remember that the way that your counseling relationships end will have a significant impact on your success as a counselor (Novick & Novick, 2006). Every counselor is ethically obligated to anticipate, plan for, and openly discuss relationship endings with clients. In fact, you should always consider termination to be a vital phase of the counseling process. Thoughtful planning related to termination protects clients' best interests in the same way that ignoring termination exposes clients to harm stemming from abrupt endings and feelings of abandonment. To adhere to the *ACA Code of Ethics* in this area *(see Standard A.11.)*, you should occasionally review the following recommendations.

Openly Discuss Termination With Clients

As part of good counseling and in an effort to protect your clients' interests *(see Standards A.11.c., A.11.d.)*, always discuss endings with clients before they occur, and allow adequate time for planning, processing, and transfer to another professional if indicated or requested by a client (Davis, 2008). Remember that achieving a successful termination will often help clients to move forward in life with greater autonomy and confidence.

Never Abandon a Client

The *ACA Code of Ethics* is very clear on this point: Counselors may not abandon clients *(see Standard A.11.a.)*. A client is likely to experience abandonment if you terminate services abruptly, refuse to return phone calls, remain unavailable between sessions, or fail to respond professionally to client emergencies. You can help to prevent abandonment by planning carefully for termination, thoroughly informing clients about procedures for contacting you or a colleague after hours or during your absence, and tailoring the termination process to the client's unique needs and clinical issues (Walsh, 2007).

Cooperate Fully in the Client Transfer Process

When a client requests or when you have highly recommended a transfer to another professional after deciding you can no longer effectively counsel a client, cooperate fully in the process. If you allow annoyance, anger, or a wounded ego to impede full cooperation when a client wishes to terminate counseling and seek a different professional, you may be in violation of Standards A.11.c. (Appropriate Termination) and A.11.d. (Appropriate Transfer of Services). Thorough cooperation includes maintaining open communication with the client and expeditiously transferring records and other information requested by the client.

Address Insurance Coverage Issues Up Front

When clients utilize their insurance or managed care company to help pay for their counseling, always verify their benefits at the outset and discuss any limitations that exist *(see Standard A.4.a.)* (Bernstein & Hartsell, 2000). Specific limits on number of sessions or rate of reimbursement must be part of the informed consent process. Clearly inform clients if the exhaustion of insurance benefits will lead to termination of counseling, transition to a sliding fee scale, or some other arrangement.

Carefully Manage Abrupt Endings

At times, a coherent termination process is not possible, such as when a client abruptly drops out of counseling. Remember that such endings do not free you from the ethical obligation to safeguard client welfare *(see Standard A.1.)* and to prevent harm to the extent possible *(see Standard A.4.)*. When a client abruptly ends services, attempt to contact him or her by phone, and if this is not successful, by letter, within a reasonable period of time. If you consider a client to be high risk (e.g., suicidal, homicidal, cognitively impaired), consider legal and ethical obligations to file a report with an appropriate agency (Barnett, MacGlashan, & Clarke, 2000). Always seek consultation concerning the balance between protecting confidentiality and preventing harm in these cases. Failing to respond to a client's abrupt termination may be seen as tacit approval. If you believe that a client requires continued counseling, be sure to communicate this clearly to the client in written form. Finally, if a client refuses further contact, you should send a final letter acknowledging termination of services and recommending, among other things, continued counseling (if this is indicated), follow-up with other professionals (such as physicians to monitor medications), emergency and crisis contact numbers, and your willingness to continue working with the client in the future if this is the case.

References

Barnett, J. E., MacGlashan, S., & Clarke, A. J. (2000). Risk management and ethical issues regarding termination and abandonment. In L. VandeCreek & T. Jackson (Eds.), *Innovations in clinical practice* (pp. 231–246). Sarasota, FL: Professional Resources Press.

Bernstein, B. E., & Hartsell, T. L. (2000). *The portable ethicist for mental health professionals: An A-Z guide to responsible practice.* New York: Wiley.

Davis, D. (2008). *Terminating therapy: A professional's guide to ending on a positive note.* Hoboken, NJ: Wiley.

Novick, J., & Novick, K. K. (2006). *Good goodbyes: Knowing how to end in psychotherapy and psychoanalysis.* Lanham, MD: Jason Aronson.

Walsh, J. (2007). *Endings in clinical practice: Effective closure in diverse settings* (2nd ed.). Chicago: Lyceum Books.

Responding to Subpoenas and Court Orders, Lawsuits, and Ethics Complaints

Learning that you have received a subpoena to appear in court, or worse, that you have been named in an ethics complaint or lawsuit, is among the more stressful experiences a counselor may encounter. Although the vast majority of counselors are never sued or named in an ethics complaint, and although receiving a subpoena may be an infrequent occurrence—depending on your area of practice—it is wise to be prepared for these events in advance.

If you are like most counselors, you might naturally experience a range of distressing emotions when confronted with a lawsuit or ethics complaint. These might include shock, denial, anxiety, anger, embarrassment, or depression, yet it is essential that you keep these emotions in check and avoid emotion-driven decisions. Even subpoenas can feel intimidating and threatening. To protect your clients and yourself, it will be important that you embark on a process of consultation, reflection, and careful decision making (Pope & Vasquez, 2007).

In the sections that follow, we offer specific step-by-step suggestions for responding to both subpoenas and lawsuits or ethics complaints.

Subpoenas and Court Orders

A subpoena is a legal document issued by an attorney that may require you to produce client records or personally appear to testify in court or give a recorded deposition in a legal matter. A court order is issued by a judge. Both must be responded to and not ignored, even if you believe it is best not to disclose the required information. It is essential that you take subpoenas and court orders seriously. In the case of a subpoena, this does not mean that you will necessarily comply with it by releasing requested records or testifying about a client's counseling. You must, however, respond to it and, if relevant, assert your client's right to privilege (the legal right to decide if confidential information is shared with others) and inform the court that you will not be releasing any requested records. In the case of a court order, which comes directly from a judge, you must comply with the order fully or risk being held in contempt of court (and possibly being fined, imprisoned, or both).

In both situations you should immediately seek consultation and make an informed decision about whether the subpoena or court order is valid (it may not even be in reference to your client), whether it is in the best interest of your client, and whether you are legally compelled to comply with it (Gross, 2001). Of course, certain kinds of counseling practice are likely to elicit more frequent subpoenas; these include forensic work, counseling with children and couples, custody evaluations, and assessment. The *ACA Code of Ethics* specifies that when you are subpoenaed to release confidential information, you should work diligently to secure your client's written consent, and when this is not possible, you must work just as diligently to prohibit this disclosure (e.g., with the assistance of your attorney) or have it limited as narrowly as possible because of potential harm to the client or the counseling relationship *(see Standard B.2.c.)*. When you receive a subpoena, it is important to review each of the following recommendations (Barsky & Gould, 2002):

- Treat the subpoena seriously—as a duly executed court document—but *do not respond immediately*. Never turn over records or make comments about any aspect of the case to the individual who serves the subpoena or to any other individual prior to consulting with your attorney.
- Consult with your attorney to determine whether the subpoena is valid and what response is required of you. It is often the case that attorneys will issue subpoenas without having any legal grounds for doing so; often a client's legal right to *privileged communication* will prevent you from having to release any records or discussing their contents. Privileged communication statutes are found in most state and federal jurisdictions. They specify that clients own a right to confidentiality that, in most legal contexts, cannot be breached without their consent (Glosoff, Herlihy, & Spence, 2000).
- When your attorney determines that a subpoena is valid, as may happen in a criminal court or when a judge has issued a court order, work with your attorney to determine the minimum level of response required; that is, how can you protect unnecessary intrusions on your client's privacy while obeying a valid legal directive to disclose confidential material?
- Carefully review the laws and statutes bearing on privileged communication in your jurisdiction so that you have a good understanding of the circumstances in which you may be legally compelled to disclose client information without client consent.
- When compelled by a valid subpoena or court order to disclose or produce confidential client information, do your best to keep your client

informed of the situation and your legal obligations. At times, a client's attorney may be helpful in quashing or nullifying a subpoena, thus eliminating the problem.

- When a subpoena is valid, consider ways to work with the originating attorney or court to limit your disclosures to only the most salient questions. At times, an attorney or judge is not entirely clear about the specific information needed. You may be able to negotiate producing a summary of the case rather than releasing all of your records. Although it will not be appropriate to delete or alter material in your record, you may be able to negotiate redactions of private material that is not entirely relevant to the legal issue in question.
- Finally, remember that the *ACA Code of Ethics* does not *require* you to follow the law when it comes to responding to subpoenas. Standard H.1.b. specifies that when laws appear to conflict with an ethical standard (e.g., avoiding harm [A.4.], respecting confidentiality [B.1.c.]), you *may* follow the law. However, you may also refuse to obey a law if this is a matter of conscience (e.g., a client would be seriously harmed by your disclosure). Of course, you must be willing to accept legal consequences such as imprisonment and monetary fines for these actions. Always consult your attorney before deciding to resist a subpoena or court order

Ethics Complaints and Lawsuits

Let's face it. Few things will be more distressing to a counselor than being named in a lawsuit or being formally charged with an ethics violation. Such news can elicit a broad range of unpleasant emotions and dysfunctional behaviors, including denial, impulsive anger, despair, and immobilization. Rather than act out in a way that you will later regret or freeze like the proverbial deer in the headlights, it will be imperative that you prepare to respond to either of these events with a deliberate and thoughtful process.

When notified of an ethics complaint or lawsuit, you should avoid any immediate response or reaction to the board, attorney, or client involved. You should notify your attorney and insurance carrier immediately. Listen carefully to your attorney and proceed carefully according to legal advice. This will also be an excellent time to seek consultation from a trusted colleague or two who can provide both moral support and professional advice relative to the complaint or lawsuit. You will need to gather all records related to the case in question and make certain that documentation is current, but do not alter the existing record in any way. It is also of paramount importance to maintain your professional self-esteem; do not let anxiety or shame about the complaint or suit cause you to engage in catastrophic (e.g., "my career is over") or self-downing (e.g., "this just proves I'm an incompetent counselor") cognitions. Keep in mind that in the case of an ethics complaint, your professional behavior will be evaluated by a jury of your peers—other counselors—who do not expect perfection in their colleagues, only meeting minimal professional standards of competence. It would be equally harmful to be nonchalant about an ethics complaint. Although it is tempting to reason that expulsion from an organization is the "worst" that can happen to you if found in violation of the *Code of Ethics*, remember that professional organizations make notifications to other organizations, including licensing boards. Expulsion or other discipline by one body may have wide-ranging effects on your ability to practice.

When you learn that you have been named in a lawsuit or ethics complaint, we recommend that you review carefully the following suggestions to guide you through the process and minimize the risk of making bad decisions in your response (Bernstein & Hartsell, 2000):

- *First, do nothing.* That is, avoid the temptation to respond immediately or impulsively when you first learn of an action against you. The last thing you want to do is to say something inflammatory or release information that may be incriminating; never make an accusation or threat that may paint you in a negative light with the court or the ethics committee. Respond politely to the conveyor of the news (e.g., attorney, licensing board, or ethics committee), and let them know that you will respond shortly.
- *Treat the complaint or lawsuit seriously, even if you know that it is entirely without merit.* At times a client or colleague may, for vindictive reasons, attempt to punish or humiliate you. At other times an impaired or distraught client may take action as one expression of his or her own pathology. Trust that these motivations will become transparent to the court or board. Remember that the *ACA Code of Ethics* requires you to cooperate fully with an ethics committee *(see Standard H.3.)*. Be certain that all of your responses to the court or a legitimate board or committee are cordial and timely.
- *Contact your attorney and your professional insurance carrier at once* (Pope & Vasquez, 2007). As soon as you have calmed yourself down and taken time to review the suggestions in the *Ethics Desk Reference for Counselors*, call your lawyer. If you have not retained an attorney with expertise in defending mental health professionals, and if your insurance carrier will not provide you with an attorney, now is the time to begin asking colleagues or professional counseling organizations for referrals. It should soon become clear which attorneys have a track record of success in this area. In nearly all cases, your insurance carrier will provide comprehensive legal consultation; if you have both an insurance company lawyer and a personal lawyer, be sure that they collaborate regarding your defense. It is never wise to attempt to represent yourself in an ethics complaint or lawsuit. Fax a copy of the complaint or lawsuit to your lawyer, and arrange a time to meet and discuss the specifics of the case and the best plan for responding.
- *Do not contact the complainant.* In nearly every instance, contacting the client or colleague who has filed the complaint or initiated the lawsuit will only make matters worse. You will come across to an ethics committee or court as badgering the client or admitting guilt. Only your legal representative should have contact with the client and his or her attorney.

- *Resist the urge to alter documentation in your records after a complaint or suit has been filed.* Organizing the existing record and adding a final entry reflecting notification of the action will ordinarily be fine, but do not attempt to add missing material or change existing documentation. Also, never attempt to destroy incriminating material in the record.
- *Be thorough in your response to the ethics charges or legal complaint.* Be comprehensive, precise, and clear in answering all of the committee's or court's questions. Being thorough conveys something of your professionalism and cooperativeness to those evaluating the merits of the case. It will often be harder for a jury, judge, or ethics committee to believe that an exceptionally conscientious counselor would knowingly behave unprofessionally.
- *Only communicate to the court, licensing board, or ethics committee through your attorney.* Even when correspondence must come from you, be sure that your attorney carefully reviews and vets your work before delivering it. As a related matter, never say anything about the case or release any record related to the case without your legal representative's explicit consent.
- *Carefully review all relevant ethical standards and state or federal laws with any relevance to the case.* Think carefully about how your ethical and legal obligations were carried out vis-à-vis the client. Be prepared to carefully articulate awareness of the *ACA Code of Ethics* and relevant statutes in your written and verbal narrative of your engagement with the client. Ethics committees and courts cannot help but be positively impressed by a thoughtful and informed analysis from the counselor's perspective.
- *Review policies and procedures.* Carefully review the policies and procedures of the ethics committee or licensing board, or in the case of a legal action, have your attorney explain court procedures, so that you grasp the process you will be facing.
- *Seek collegial consultation and support.* It is often profoundly helpful and reassuring to ask one or two trusted colleagues to provide you with moral support, friendship, and consultation when going through the experience. Although you must be careful not to reveal details about the case that would violate confidentiality, it will often be deeply affirming and encouraging to have colleagues available to check in with you routinely for support (Chauvin & Remley, 1996).
- *Practice self-care.* Weathering the stress of an ethics complaint or lawsuit can be difficult in the best of circumstances. Consider personal counseling or supervision, and be sure to attend to good nutrition, exercise, and sleep so that you are prepared to handle the many microstressors that may emerge along the way (Chauvin & Remley, 1996).

References

Barsky, A. E., & Gould, J. W. (2002). *Clinicians in court: A guide to subpoenas, depositions, testifying, and everything else you need to know.* New York: Guilford Press.

Bernstein, B. E., & Hartsell, T. L., Jr. (2000). *The portable ethicist for mental health professionals: An A-Z guide to responsible practice.* Hoboken, NJ: Wiley.

Chauvin, J. C., & Remley, T. P., Jr. (1996). Responding to allegations of unethical conduct. *Journal of Counseling & Development, 74,* 563–568.

Glosoff, H. L., Herlihy, B., & Spence, E. B. (2000). Privileged communication in the counselor–client relationship. *Journal of Counseling & Development, 78,* 454–462.

Gross, B. H. (2001). Protecting yourself when subpoenaed: Reaching beyond client records. *The Forensic Examiner, 10,* 29–30.

Pope, K. S., & Vasquez, M. J. T. (2007). *Ethics in psychotherapy and counseling: A practical guide* (3rd ed.). San Francisco: Jossey-Bass.

Appendix

Resources for Counselors

Ethics Web Pages

American Counseling Association (ACA)
http://www.counseling.org/

Available ACA downloads include:

Multicultural Counseling Competencies and Standards
Cross-Cultural Competencies and Objectives
Advocacy Competencies
Association for Specialists in Group Work Best Practice Guidelines
Definition of Professional Counseling

ACA Ethics Resources
http://www.counseling.org/Resources/CodeOfEthics/TP/Home/CT2.aspx

Information on consulting with the ACA Professional Affairs staff regarding ethical issues and dilemmas. E-mail them directly at ethics@counseling.org.

Download the *ACA Code of Ethics*
Continuing Education on Counselor Ethics
Ethics Update and Resources
Policies and Procedures for Processing Complaints of Ethical Violations

ACA's Private Practice Pointers
http://www.counseling.org/Counselors/PrivatePracticePointers.aspx

American Mental Health Counselors Association *Code of Ethics*
http://www.amhca.org/code/

American School Counselor Association *Ethical Standards for School Counselors*
http://www.schoolcounselor.org/content.asp?contentid=173

Association for Counselor Education and Supervision *Ethical Guidelines for Counseling Supervisors*
http://www.acesonline.net/ethical_guidelines.asp

Canadian Counselling Association *Code of Ethics*
http://www.ccacc.ca/e_COE.html

Council for Accreditation of Counseling and Related Educational Programs *2009 Standards*
http://www.cacrep.org/2009standards.html

Ethical Decision Making
http://www.scu.edu/ethics/practicing/decision/

Ethical Decision Making and Dual Relationships
http://kspope.com/dual/younggren.php

Ethics and Malpractice
http://kspope.com/ethics/index.php

Informed Consent in Psychotherapy and Counseling: Forms, Standards and Guidelines, and References
http://kspope.com/consent/index.php

National Board for Certified Counselors
http://www.nbcc.org/

National Board for Certified Counselors *Code of Ethics*
http://www.nbcc.org/AssetManagerFiles/ethics/nbcc-codeofethics.pdf

A Practitioner's Guide to Ethical Decision Making (a publication of the ACA)
http://www.counseling.org/Files/FD.ashx?guid=c4dcf247-66e8-45a3-abcc-024f5d7e836f

Therapist's Guide for Preparing a Professional Will
http://kspope.com/therapistas/will.php

Federal Laws

Child Abuse Reporting Laws for All States
http://www.childwelfare.gov/systemwide/laws_policies/state/can/

Family Educational Rights and Privacy Act (FERPA)
http://www.ed.gov/policy/gen/reg/ferpa/index.html

Health Insurance Portability and Accountability Act (HIPAA)
http://www.hhs.gov/ocr/hipaa/

Selected Books on Ethics

Corey, G., Corey, M. S., & Callanan, P. (2007). *Issues and ethics in the helping professions* (7th ed.). Belmont, CA: Brooks Cole.

Cottone, R. R., & Tarvydas, V. M. (2007). *Counseling ethics and decision-making* (3rd ed.). Upper Saddle River, NJ: Pearson Education.

Herlihy, B., & Corey, G. (2006). *ACA ethical standards casebook* (6th ed.). Alexandria, VA: American Counseling Association.

Herlihy, B., & Corey, G. (2006). *Boundary issues in counseling: Multiple roles and responsibilities* (2nd ed.). Alexandria, VA: American Counseling Association.

Ingersoll, R. E., & Welfel, E. R. (2004). *The mental health desk reference: A practice-based guide to diagnosis, treatment, and professional ethics.* Hoboken, NJ: Wiley.

Johnson, W. B., & Ridley, C. R. (2008). *The elements of ethics.* New York: Palgrave Macmillan.

Pope, K. S., Sonne, J. L., & Greene, B. (2006). *What therapists don't talk about and why: Understanding taboos that hurt us and our clients.* Washington, DC: American Psychological Association.

Pope, K. S., & Vasquez, M. J. T. (2007). *Ethics in psychotherapy and counseling: A practical guide* (3rd ed.). San Francisco: Jossey-Bass.

Welfel, E. R. (2005). *Ethics in counseling and psychotherapy: Standards, research, and emerging issues.* Washington, DC: Thompson Brooks/Cole.

Wheeler, A. M., & Bertram, B. (2008). *The counselor and the law* (5th ed.). Alexandria, VA: American Counseling Association.

Continuing Education for Counselors

Each of the following offers home study continuing education in ethics and ethical practice for counselors:

- ACA Online Learning: http://www.counseling.org/Resources/Online-Learning.aspx
- AtHealth.Com: http://www.athealthce.com/
- CE4Less.com: http://www.ce4less.com/index.aspx
- ContinuingEdCourses.Net: http://www.continuingedcourses.net/
- National Association for Continuing Education: http://www.naceonline.com
- Professional Resource Press: http://www.prpress.com/ce.html
- Psy Broadcasting Corporation (PsyBC): http://www.psybc.com/
- Zur Institute: http://www.drzur.com/

Index

A

D

E

F

G

H

I

J

K

L

M

N

O

P

Q

R

S

T

U

V

W

HOLY FAMILY UNIV LIBRARY
3 1070 00069 9112

Holy Family
UNIVERSITY